THE WORKS OF SHAKESPEARE

EDITED FOR THE SYNDICS OF THE
CAMBRIDGE UNIVERSITY PRESS
BY
SIR ARTHUR QUILLER-COUCH
AND   JOHN DOVER WILSON

THE
TWO GENTLEMEN
OF VERONA

THE
TWO GENTLEMEN
OF VERONA

CAMBRIDGE

AT THE UNIVERSITY PRESS

1969

PUBLISHED BY
THE SYNDICS OF THE CAMBRIDGE UNIVERSITY PRESS

Bentley House, 200 Euston Road, London, N.W. 1
American Branch: 32 East 57th Street, New York, N.Y. 10022

Standard Book Number:
521 07562 9 clothbound
521 09505 0 paperback

First edition 1921
*Reprinted 1955
First paperback edition 1969

* Places where editorial changes or additions intro-
duce variants from the first edition are, where possible, marked by a date [1955] in square brackets.

First printed in Great Britain at the University Press, Cambridge
Reprinted in Great Britain by Hazell Watson & Viney Ltd,
Aylesbury, Bucks

CONTENTS

CONTENTS

THE TWO GENTLEMEN OF VERONA

So far as we know, this play first achieved print in the Folio of 1623, where it follows *The Tempest*. But it stands first on the list of six comedies mentioned by Meres in 1598; and all internal tests, of craftsmanship and versification, point to a date considerably earlier yet. It is indeed, by general consent, a youthful production: and we may pretty safely place it somewhere near the threshold of Shakespeare's dramatic career.

At all events, in the long interval before the stage copy reached the Folio printers the theatrical people had played some strange tricks upon it. Shakespeare's original carelessness may perhaps have been to blame for mixing up Verona and Padua with Milan[1], as for giving Verona a roadstead and starting Valentine for Milan—as easily as one might start him from Oxford to Cambridge—by sea. Shakespeare, first and last, was sadly addicted to finishing off a play in a hurry. But the final scene of the *Two Gentlemen* is vitiated (as we hope to show) by a flaw too unnatural to be charged upon Shakespeare.

Reserving this, and putting the vexation of it out of our thought for the moment, we can enjoy the play as a light and jocund Italianate comedy—Italianate, that is, in the Elizabethan fashion, when it chose to take its Italy gaily. For Italy was the traditional, almost conventional, scene of Elizabethan drama, and could be taken either way— with vice and murder, Borgia cups, daggers, tortures and intellectual refinements of depravity (with its 'blackguard quality air.' to use Carlyle's phrase of King John), or with masks, mandolins and pretty amorous intrigue. Verona serves as background for Julia and for

[1] See notes on 2. 5. 1; 3. 1. 81; 5. 4. 130.

Juliet; Venice for Shylock and for Othello as handily as for Gratiano; and Launce and Launcelot Gobbo are brothers and might inhabit either. In the original version of that most English of comedies, *Every Man in his Humour*, Jonson laid the scene in Florence and gave his characters Italian names. Few will deny that by transferring the scene to London and turning his eccentrics into English men and women he made—by this process alone—a vastly better play; that in his native-grown Comedy of Humours this increase of realism increases his vivacity and verisimilitude. The audience approved, and the successors and congeners of *Every Man in his Humour*—*Epicoene*, *The Alchemist*, *Bartholomew's Fair*—were duly located in or near London.

> Our *Scene* is *London*, 'cause we would make knowne
> No countries mirth is better then our owne....
>
> (Prologue to *The Alchemist*, 1610.)

The apology, however, hints the innovation. In 1598 Jonson would stage his British comedy in Florence as unhesitatingly as, ten years or so later, Webster staged his Italianate *White Devil* in Rome or Padua; or—shall we say?—with no more trouble of artistic conscience than Shakespeare felt in dodging the centuries and dragging the right Renaissance scoundrel Iachimo into a supposed early-British *Tragedie of Cymbeline*. 'Somewhere in Italy' was in fact the spot where an Elizabethan playwright and his audience started upon agreed terms. Apart from the tradition and the romance of it, this convention of Italy conveniently accommodated the players, under a wide range of magnificent titles, with a still wider wardrobe of magnificent and miscellaneous costumes.

Guess-work suggests that in *The Two Gentlemen of Verona* Shakespeare recast an old lost play *The History of Felix and Philiomena*, entered in the Revels Accounts, 1584–5, as having been acted by the Queen's company at Greenwich 'on the sondaie next after neweyeares daie at night': because the Proteus and Julia story comes straight out of an episodic tale in a Spanish romance, *Los siete libros de la Diana*, written by a Portuguese, Jorge de Montemayor, and translated by Bartholomew Yonge; and because the names in the title of this lost play repeat (with allowance made for a copyist's error) the names of the hero, 'Felix,' and the heroine, 'Felismena,' of Montemayor's story. Felix woos Felismena by letter with her maid as intermediary; he travels to Court and is pursued by Felismena in male attire; she lodges at an inn, overhears him serenading another mistress, takes service with him as a page—the recognition being effected later after a scene of combat in a forest. There are other points of resemblance, but these may suffice.

We shall get more instruction perhaps—as we shall certainly get more amusement—from looking forward than from casting back. For *The Two Gentlemen of Verona* holds a store of stage-effects which Shakespeare kept henceforth in his locker, to try them and to improve on them again and again. For a few examples—

(1) It would seem that he was already acquainted with George Brooke's poem of *Romeus and Juliet* (1562): for our play anticipates *Romeo and Juliet* (based upon that poem) in a number of particulars—the place, Verona; Silvia's window and balcony, most like Juliet's; the rope-ladder which Valentine has patented ahead of Romeo. Juliet makes assignation at 'Friar Laurence' cell'; but Silvia has been beforehand with her

> at Friar Patrick's cell
> Where I intend holy confession—

and (as Fluellen might say) there is a Friar Laurence in both. Valentine's burden of despair on the word 'banished' preludes Romeo's descant[1]:

> There is no world without Verona walls
> But purgatory, torture, hell itself.

[1] v. note on 3. 1. 170–87.

> Hence-banishéd is banished from the world,
> And world's exile is death: then banishéd
> Is death mis-termed...

—and so on, through a score of suggestions and echoes.

(2) But when we come to *The Merchant of Venice* these echoes multiply. We have already noted the brotherly likeness between Launce and Launcelot Gobbo. It is a trifle in comparison with the scenes in which Julia and Portia discuss choice of suitors with their maids; a trifle when we consider the number of heroines Shakespeare set travelling after Julia in man's attire: Rosalind, Viola, Imogen and every single woman in *The Merchant of Venice*—Portia, Jessica, Nerissa. On a minor point, we may compare the use of the ring-token to bring about 'recognition' in these two plays.

The mission of the disguised Julia to Silvia is repeated and beautifully improved in *Twelfth Night*. The outlaw business is worked better and better in successive plays. Speed's discourse on the marks of a lover is father of a numerous progeny....But we have said enough, and need not extend the list.

We may, then (still bating the last scene), read in *The Two Gentlemen* something more than a graceful story charmingly told. It is that: but it also fixes and holds in arrest for us a fleet youthful and peculiarly fascinating phase or moment in the efflorescence of Shakespeare's art:

> For ever warm and still to be enjoyed,
> For ever panting and for ever young!

and our pleasure in studying it, though we have begun with dramatic 'effects,' by no means ends with them.

The diction is melodious, on the whole too mellifluous. 'Fine writing' still engages him, and a butterfly 'conceit' still allures him to pursue and over-run it. Lucetta has already (I. 2. 30) announced of love that

> Fire that's closest kept burns most of all—

and Julia elaborates this later (2. 7. 24) into

> The more thou damm'st it up, the more it burns:
> The current that with gentle murmur glides,
> Thou know'st, being stopped, impatiently doth rage:
> But when his fair course is not hinderéd
> He makes sweet music with th'enamelled stones,
> Giving a gentle kiss to every sedge
> He overtaketh in his pilgrimage;
> And so by many winding nooks he strays,
> With willing sport, to the wide ocean....

We all remember the passage for its imagery, its cadence, and its delicately chosen words. But it is boyish, inexperienced: it keeps the speaker dallying luxuriously with an image while the dramatic moment slips away; the passion requisite for fusing the two having had time to cool. It is pretty: but it has not the masterly touch of

> And unregarded age in corners thrown

or

> O liméd soul, that struggling to be free
> Art more engaged! Help, angels! make assay...

or

> The lamentable change is from the best;
> The worst returns to laughter.

For promise of that, to find it in *The Two Gentlemen*, we must seek among chance lines:

> Poor wounded name: my bosom, as a bed,
> Shall lodge thee till thy wound be throughly healed.

> Wilt thou reach stars, because they shine on thee?

> Who should be trusted, when one's own right hand
> Is perjured to the bosom?

But the promise is there.

There is notable promise, too, in the characters. *The Two Gentlemen* would seem to be the earliest play in which Shakespeare turned from 'construction'—that idol of artistic beginners—to weld character into his plot. Again as in *The Comedy of Errors* he gives us two gentle-

men with a servant apiece: but this time he discriminates
master from master, servant from servant, to individualise
them. To be sure, because he has to follow a ready-made
story, we find him experimenting most happily upon the
characters—upon Launce, for example—who give him
most liberty because they are least tied to obey the
exigencies of the intrigue. Proteus has to play the almost
incredibly false friend, in order to work the story; and to
make it plausible, even to himself, must spend most of his
time and ours upon cold sophistries. Valentine and Silvia
have been well called 'two silver-point studies,' 'somewhat high-fantastical, but gentleman and lady to the
core.' The plot allows them high moments of generosity—
nay, even works upon these—yet in its motion treats the
pair as dupes, almost as dummies. For example, it is
not by proof or by prowess that Valentine becomes
captain of the outlaws, but simply because they like
his looks and accept his bare word for his linguistic
attainments.

Nevertheless, and throughout the play, we feel that
Shakespeare, though—with the exceptions of Julia and
Launce—he cannot, without making them dull, keep
any of his *dramatis personae* steadily *consistent*, is always
keeping them lively and always bringing them to the edge,
at least, of startling us by some individuality. We feel, as
we read, that these people are impatient of the convention within which they are held: that any one of them,
at any moment, may break out and do something
original; and this holds us in an atmosphere of ex-
pectancy which, if not the same as reality, curiously
resembles it. Yet while individualising these people, he
is learning to give them—the women especially—that
catholic kinship which communicates to us, as we wander
in Shakespeare's great portrait gallery, a delightful sense
of intimacy, of recognition. They belong to a family—our
family—the Human Family. For this trick of feature (we
have already compared Julia and Lucetta with Portia and

Nerissa, discussing suitors) let us take Silvia's hesitancy in handing back Valentine's letter:

Silvia. Yes, yes: the lines are very quaintly writ,
But—since unwillingly—take them again...
Nay, take them.
Valentine.   Madam, they are for you.
Silvia. Ay, ay: you writ them, sir, at my request,
But I will none of them: they are for you:
I would have had them writ more movingly...

                                        [*he takes the letter*
Valentine. Please you, I'll write your ladyship another.
Silvia. And when it's writ...for my sake read it over,
And, if it please you, so...if not...why, so...
Valentine. If it please me, madam, what then?
Silvia. Why, if it please you, take it for your labour;
And so good-morrow, servant.

and let us, bearing it in mind, cast forward to Beatrice's feminine hesitancy in *Much Ado about Nothing*:

Benedick. I do love nothing in the world so well as you— is not that strange?
Beatrice. As strange as the thing I know not. It were as possible for me to say I loved nothing so well as you, but believe me not, and yet I lie not, I confess nothing, nor I deny nothing, I am sorry for my cousin[1].

We come now to the final scene, and, in particular, to the passage which has offended so many critics of sensibility: the lines in which Valentine 'empties'—as the Germans say—'the baby with the bath,' and, after pardoning his false friend, proceeds to give away (in every sense) his most loyal lady-love to her would-be ravisher. Here they are, as printed in the Folio:

Pro. My shame and guilt confounds me:
Forgiue me *Valentine*: if hearty sorrow
Be a sufficient Ransome for offence,
I tender't heere: I doe as truely suffer,
As ere I did commit.

---

[1] The Folio allows no stop heavier than a comma to the hurry of this speech.

Val. Then I am paid:
And once again, I doe receive thee honest;
Who by Repentance is not satisfied,
Is nor of heauen, nor earth; for these are pleas'd:
By Penitence th' Eternalls wrath's appeas'd:
And that my loue may appeare plaine and free,
All that was mine, in *Siluia*, I give thee.
Jul. Oh me unhappy.
Pro. Looke to the Boy.
Val. Why, Boy?
Why wag: how now? what's the matter? look vp:
    speak.

'All that was mine in Silvia I give thee'—one's impulse,
upon this declaration, is to remark that there are, by this
time, *no* gentlemen in Verona.

We must not, without a second thought, pronounce
that this and the preceding line are not Shakespeare's—
could not have been written by Shakespeare. They are
uncouth: but he wrote, first and last, many uncouth lines,
and his present editors will not challenge an obvious
retort by making affidavit of their private conviction—
firm though it be—that he never wrote these. They are
dramatically inconsistent: they disappoint all that we
suppose ourselves to know of Valentine's character, and
so unexpectedly that we feel it like a slap in the face. But
again it is not quite enough to say

That he could have deliberately set himself to mar, in this
concluding scene, his two silver-point studies of Valentine
and Silvia, those may believe who will. That he could have
done it, and not known what he was doing, is incredible.

adding that if he really intended it,

Why, we are left face to face with a mistake in art, an
offence against dramatic propriety, which has no distant
resemblance to anything else that is Shakespeare's. It is
not a matter of youthful inexperience: there is no plausibility
in the forlorn suggestion that he was imitating the faults of
older dramatists. The couplet is no part of his conception[1].

[1] Sir George Young in *The Reading University College
Review*, vol. VII. No. 19.

For mediaeval and Renaissance writers had a fashion with Friendship: a literary convention of refining, ideal-ising, exalting it out of all proportion, or at any rate above the proportion it bears, in our modern minds, either to love between man and woman or to parental love. We see it perhaps at its most extravagant in the famous story of *Amis and Amile*, in which Amile at the command of an angel slays his two children that their blood may wash Amis free of leprosy: but we realise it better in Montaigne, balancing his avowals of affection for Étienne de la Boëtie against anything and everything he says of marital love: for in the *Essays* we have this disproportion homelily, cheerfully, reduced to matter-of-fact and taken for granted. But we need not seek even beyond Shakespeare. That the convention lay strong upon him no one can doubt who studies the Sonnets, or weighs the claims of friendship and love in *The Merchant of Venice*. 'Shall we say, then,' writes Dowden, of this passage, 'that Shakespeare was here sacrificing truth and nature to a convention of the time?' Or may we rather admit that, after all, there *is* some plausibility in 'the forlorn suggestion' that he was—not 'imitating the faults of older dramatists'—but working on an old play; and that, in the end, after re-furbishing the story and making its characters life-like, he found himself faced with a conventional *dénouement* and closed the account with a tag of doggerel either contemptuously invented or transferred literally from the *corpus vile*?

It is possible: and we will give a devil's advocate yet a little farther scope. There is a tradition (which we are unable to trace to its source) that *The Two Gentlemen of Verona* proved a failure on the stage. If so, nothing in the play would account for it so easily as this most crucial blunder.

Allowing something—not too much, we think—to this tradition, we offer another hypothesis: first asking the reader to turn to our Note on the Copy for *The Two*

Gentlemen of Verona, pp. 77–82 of this volume (noting especially pp. 79–81), where he will find our reasons for believing that the botcher's hand—or, may be, the hands of several botchers—may be detected in our text and throughout it. But here we deal with the most flagrant and vitiating passage, and suggest a possible explanation—there is no possible excuse. It may be, then, that Shakespeare invented a solution which at the first performance was found to be ineffective; that the final scene was partly re-written—not by Shakespeare—and given its crude and conventional *coup de théâtre*; that in this mutilated form it remained on the play-copy; and that so it reached the printer. We believe, at any rate, that no one can re-read *this* scene carefully without detecting that pieces of it are Shakespeare's and other pieces have been inserted by a 'faker' who not only was not Shakespeare, but did not possess even a rudimentary ear for blank verse. The opening lines bewray him:

1 *Outlaw*. Come, come, be patient: we must bring you
   to our captain.
Silvia. A thousand more mischances than this one
Have learned me how to brook this patiently.
2 *Outlaw*. Come, bring her away.
1 *Outlaw*. Where is the gentleman that was with her?
3 *Outlaw*. Being nimble-footed, he hath outrun us.
But Moses and Valerius follow him:
Go thou with her to the west end of the wood,
There is our captain: we'll follow him that's fled.

Shakespeare's prosody is often easy-going, and not seldom—to a pedantic mind—perverse: but to our ear it is never slipshod or vicious *in that way*. And this faultiness exactly coincides with a significant, if a minor, fault of dramatic craftsmanship—the damnation of Sir Eglamour's taking-off. Sir Eglamour—not to be confused with the knight of that name who figures among Julia's suitors in Act i, Scene 2[1]—has obviously been

---

[1] But cf. note I. 2. 9.

dragged into the plot by no fault of his own. He is just an honest, simple gentleman on whose chivalry Silvia makes claim for help in a most difficult adventure.

> O Eglamour, thou art a gentleman...
> Upon whose faith and honour I repose.

His answer is prompt, as his service is punctual. Without warning or excuse he is reported to have taken to his heels like the veriest poltroon! At once, helped by muddled versification, we perceive that this scene is running agley, that some interposing hand is murdering the verse along with dramatic consistency. Amid lines that have Shakespeare's trick and cadence are thrust strange ones that no ear can accept for his. Suddenly, with the crisis, we come upon the doggerel:

> And that my love may appear plain and free,
> All that was mine in Silvia I give thee.

Having noted the jingle which follows on the rhyme of 'pleased' and 'appeased,' we note further that there is only one other instance in this melodiously written play of an unrhymed speech finished off with two rhymed couplets; and that is the very speech (uttered by Proteus) which, if it have any meaning at all, improves in caddishness upon Valentine's offence:

> O heaven, were man
> But constant, he were perfect; that one error
> Fills him with faults...

—so far Shakespeare, perhaps: now for cacophony followed by nonsense:

> makes him run through all th'sins;
> Inconstancy falls off ere it begins:
> What is in Silvia's face, but I may spy
> More fresh in Julia's *with a constant eye*?

Can anyone believe Shakespeare guilty of this pair of tags: the first lame in scansion and unmeaning, the second balanced for our choice between nonsense and rascality?

And where is Silvia in all this business? She is merely left. She utters not a word after Valentine's pseudo-magnificent, pseudo-romantic, renunciation. 'A curious essay,' says Dowden, 'might be written upon the silences of some of the characters of Shakespeare.' It would be an ingenious one if it could account for Silvia's silence here save by the alternatives, *either* of her being sick and tired of both her lovers, *or* of the whole scene's being (as we submit) a piece of theatre botchwork patched upon the original.

But it will be asked, if we omit

> All that was mine in Silvia I give thee

—how do we account for Julia's swoon? Our own answer is that we do not try to account for it: our hypothesis being that the swoon and the couplet together are 'other man's work'; that Shakespeare had another *dénouement* which possibly proved ineffective on the stage, and that the one we have is a stage-adapter's substitute. To be sure, the stage-direction 'faints' or 'swoons' is an interpolation, not found in the Folio (which, in the text of this play, provides no stage-directions): but it seems to be required by the context *as the passage stands*. Sir George Young surmises that Julia does not really swoon but shams swooning. He holds Julia to be, in comparison with Silvia, something of an ordinary wench; that she and Proteus together are portrayed as 'lovers of common clay, of less than second-rate refinement,' meant to be a foil to chivalrous Valentine and Silvia. On our reading of the play we dissent: we really must divorce Julia from Proteus at this point. But we think it fair to give his interpretation:

> ...Julia had all her quick and rather vulgar wits about her. She thinks her little romance has been in the background long enough. She heaves a deep sigh and throws herself on the grass. This she does, as she proceeds directly to explain, because she has 'forgotten' to give Silvia the ring which

Silvia has positively refused to receive from her. She then proceeds to play off on Proteus the same sly little game, of handing him the wrong ring, which she had already tried and found superfluous with Silvia, when she handed her the wrong letter. Her demeanour is an obvious make-up, to attract attention and lead to the recognition for which she has become impatient.

This *may*—though we doubt it—interpret the passage as it stands. But it offends against our opinion of Julia: and, for the rest, we content ourselves with the questions we have raised on the scene. We know that when Shakespeare was old enough, and craftsman enough, to devise the 'recognition' in the last scene of *Cymbeline*, with its

Why did you throw your wedded lady from you?

he could do better: and we believe that even in *The Two Gentlemen* he wrote something which, if theatrically ineffective, was better, because more natural, than the text allows us to know.

[1921]   Q.

TO THE READER

The following is a brief description of the punctuation and other typographical devices employed in the text, which have been more fully explained in the *Note on Punctuation* and the *Textual Introduction* to be found in *The Tempest* volume:

An obelisk (†) implies corruption or emendation, and suggests a reference to the Notes.

A single bracket at the beginning of a speech signifies an 'aside.'

Four dots represent a full-stop in the original, except when it occurs at the end of a speech, and they mark a long pause.

Original colons or semicolons, which denote a somewhat shorter pause, are retained, or represented as three dots when they appear to possess special dramatic significance.

Similarly, significant commas have been given as dashes.

Round brackets are taken from the original, and mark a significant change of voice; when the original brackets seem to imply little more than the drop in tone accompanying parenthesis, they are conveyed by commas or dashes.

In plays for which both Folio and Quarto texts exist, passages taken from the text not selected as the basis for the present edition will be enclosed within square brackets.

Single inverted commas (' ') are editorial; double ones (" ") derive from the original, where they are used to draw attention to maxims, quotations, etc.

The reference number for the first line is given at the head of each page. Numerals in square brackets are placed at the beginning of the traditional acts and scenes.

THE TWO GENTLEMEN
OF VERONA

The scene: Verona, Milan and a forest
near Milan

CHARACTERS IN THE PLAY

DUKE OF MILAN, *father to Silvia*

VALENTINE ⎫
PROTEUS ⎬ *the two gentlemen*

ANTONIO, *father to Proteus*

THURIO, *a foolish rival to Valentine*

EGLAMOUR, *agent for Silvia in her escape*

SPEED, *a clownish servant to Valentine*

LAUNCE, *the like to Proteus*

PANTHINO, *servant to Antonio*

Host, *where Julia lodges*

Outlaws, *with Valentine*

JULIA, *beloved of Proteus*

SILVIA, *beloved of Valentine*

LUCETTA, *waiting-woman to Julia*

Servants, musicians

THE TWO GENTLEMEN
OF VERONA

Verona: a street near Julia's house;
trees and a seat

VALENTINE, dressed for a journey: PROTEUS

Valentine. Cease to persuade, my loving Proteus;
Home-keeping youth have ever homely wits.
Were't not affection chains thy tender days
To the sweet glances of thy honoured love,
I rather would entreat thy company
To see the wonders of the world abroad,
Than, living dully sluggardized at home,
Wear out thy youth with shapeless idleness....
But, since thou lov'st; love still and thrive therein,
Even as I would when I to love begin.   10

Proteus. Wilt thou be gone? Sweet Valentine, adieu.
Think on thy Proteus, when thou—haply—seest
Some rare note-worthy object in thy travel....
Wish me partaker in thy happiness,
When thou dost meet good hap; and in thy danger—
If ever danger do environ thee—
Commend thy grievance to my holy prayers,
For I will be thy beadsman, Valentine.

Valentine. And on a love-book pray for my success!

Proteus. Upon some book I love I'll pray for thee.   20

Valentine. That's on some shallow story of deep love,
How young Leander crossed the Hellespont.

Proteus. That's a deep story of a deeper love,
For he was more than over-shoes in love.

Valentine. 'Tis true; for you are over-boots in love,
And yet you never swam the Hellespont.

Proteus. Over the boots? nay, give me not the boots.
Valentine. No, I will not; for it boots thee not.
Proteus.   What?
Valentine. To be in love; where scorn is bought
30   with groans:
Coy looks, with heart-sore sighs: one fading mo-
    ment's mirth,
With twenty watchful, weary, tedious nights;
If haply won, perhaps a hapless gain;
If lost, why then a grievous labour won;
How ever...but a folly bought with wit,
Or else a wit by folly vanquishéd.
    Proteus. So, by your circumstance, you call me fool.
    Valentine. So, by your circumstance, I fear, you'll prove
    Proteus. 'Tis Love you cavil at. I am not Love.
    Valentine. Love is your master, for he masters you;
40 And he that is so yokéd by a fool,
Methinks should not be chronicled for wise.
    Proteus. Yet writers say; As in the sweetest bud
The eating canker dwells, so eating love
Inhabits in the finest wits of all.
    Valentine. And writers say; As the most forward bud
Is eaten by the canker ere it blow,
Even so by love the young and tender wit
Is turned to folly—blasting in the bud,
Losing his verdure even in the prime,
50 And all the fair effects of future hopes....
But wherefore waste I time to counsel thee
That art a votary to fond desire?
Once more adieu: my father at the road
Expects my coming, there to see me shipped.
    Proteus. And thither will I bring thee, Valentine.
    Valentine. Sweet Proteus, no: now let us take our leave;
To Milan let me hear from thee by letters

Of thy success in love; and what news else
Betideth here in absence of thy friend:
And I likewise will visit thee with mine.　　　60
　Proteus. All happiness bechance to thee in Milan.
　Valentine. As much to you at home: and so, farewell.
　　　　　　　[*they embrace and Valentine goes his way*
　Proteus. He after honour hunts, I after love;
He leaves his friends, to dignify them more;
I leave myself, my friends, and all for love...
Thou, Julia, thou hast metamorphosed me:
Made me neglect my studies, lose my time;
War with good counsel; set the world at nought;
Made wit with musing, weak; heart sick with thought.

　　　SPEED runs up breathless, carrying luggage

　Speed. Sir Proteus...'save you...saw you my master?　　70
　Proteus. But now he parted hence to embark for Milan.
　Speed. Twenty to one then he is shipped already,
And I have played the sheep in losing him.
　Proteus. Indeed a sheep doth very often stray,
An if the shepherd be awhile away.
　Speed. You conclude that my master is a shepherd then,
　　and I a sheep?
　Proteus. I do.
　Speed. Why then my horns are his horns, whether I wake
　　or sleep.
　Proteus. A silly answer, and fitting well a sheep.
　Speed. This proves me still a sheep.　　　　　80
　Proteus. True: and thy master a shepherd.
　Speed. Nay, that I can deny by a circumstance.
　Proteus. It shall go hard but I'll prove it by another.
　Speed. The shepherd seeks the sheep, and not the sheep
the shepherd; but I seek my master, and my master seeks
not me: therefore I am no sheep.

Proteus. The sheep for fodder follow the shepherd, the shepherd for food follows not the sheep: thou for wages followest thy master, thy master for wages follows not
90 thee: therefore thou art a sheep.

Speed. Such another proof will make me cry 'baa.'

Proteus. But dost thou hear? gav'st thou my letter to Julia?

Speed. Ay, sir: I, a lost mutton, gave your letter to her, a laced mutton, and she, a laced mutton, gave me, a lost mutton, nothing for my labour.

Proteus. Here's too small a pasture for such store of muttons.

Speed. If the ground be overcharged, you were best
100 stick her.

Proteus. Nay, in that you are a-stray...'twere best pound you.

Speed. Nay sir, less than a pound shall serve me for carrying your letter.

Proteus. You mistake; I mean the pound, a pinfold.

Speed. From a pound to a pin—fold it over and over, 'Tis threefold too little for carrying a letter to your lover.

Proteus. †But what said she? [*Speed nods*] Nod?

Speed. Ay.

110 *Proteus.* Nod-ay, why that's noddy.

Speed. You mistook, sir: I say she did nod; and you ask me if she did nod, and I say, 'Ay.'

Proteus. And that set together, is 'noddy.'

Speed. Now you have taken the pains to set it together, take it for your pains.

Proteus. No, no, you shall have it for bearing the letter.

Speed. Well, I perceive I must be fain to bear with you.

Proteus. Why, sir, how do you bear with me?

Speed. Marry sir, the letter very orderly—having nothing
120 but the word 'noddy' for my pains.

Proteus. Beshrew me, but you have a quick wit.

Speed. And yet it cannot overtake your slow purse.

Proteus. Come, come, open the matter in brief; what said she?

Speed. Open your purse, that the money and the matter may be both at once delivered.

Proteus. Well, sir: [*giving him money*] here is for your pains...What said she?

Speed [*eyeing the coin with contempt*]. Truly sir, I think you'll hardly win her.   130

Proteus. Why! couldst thou perceive so much from her?

Speed. Sir, I could perceive nothing at all from her;
No, not so much as a ducat for delivering your letter:
And being so hard to me that brought your mind;
I fear she'll prove as hard to you in telling your mind....
Give her no token but stones, for she's as hard as steel.

Proteus. What, said she—nothing?

Speed [*dryly*]. No, not so much as 'Take this for thy pains'... To testify your bounty, I thank you, you have   140
testerned me; in requital whereof, henceforth carry your letters yourself; and so, sir, I'll commend you to my master.   [*he swaggers off*

Proteus [*angry*]. Go, go, be gone, to save your ship
    from wrack,
Which cannot perish having thee aboard,
Being destined to a drier death on shore...
I must go send some better messenger.
I fear my Julia would not deign my lines,
Receiving them from such a worthless post.   [*he goes*

[I.2.] *A door opens:* JULIA *and* LUCETTA *come forth*

Julia. But say, Lucetta—now we are alone—
Wouldst thou then counsel me to fall in love?

Lucetta. Ay madam, so you stumble not unheedfully.

Julia [*sits*]. Of all the fair resort of gentlemen

That every day with parle encounter me,

In thy opinion which is worthiest love?

Lucetta. Please you repeat their names, I'll show my mind

According to my shallow simple skill.

Julia. What think'st thou of the fair Sir Eglamour?

10   *Lucetta.* As of a knight, well-spoken, neat, and fine;

But, were I you, he never should be mine.

Julia. What think'st thou of the rich Mercatio?

Lucetta. Well of his wealth; but of himself, so, so.

Julia [*looks down*]. What think'st thou of the gentle
     Proteus?

Lucetta. Lord, lord...to see what folly reigns in us!

Julia [*sharply*]. How now! what means this passion at
     his name?

Lucetta [*demure*]. Pardon, dear madam—'tis a pass-
     ing shame,

That I (unworthy body as I am!)

Should censure thus on lovely gentlemen.

20   *Julia.* Why not on Proteus, as of all the rest?

Lucetta. Then thus...of many good I think him best.

Julia. Your reason?

Lucetta. I have no other but a woman's reason:

I think him so, because I think him so.

Julia. And wouldst thou have me cast my love
     on him?

Lucetta. Ay...if you thought your love not cast away.

Julia. Why, he, of all the rest, hath never moved me.

Lucetta. Yet he, of all the rest, I think best loves ye.

Julia. His little speaking shows his love but small.

30   *Lucetta.* Fire, that's closest kept, burns most of all.

Julia. They do not love, that do not show their love

Lucetta. O they love least, that let men know their love

Julia.   I would, I knew his mind.
Lucetta.   Peruse this paper, madam.   [*Julia takes it*
Julia.   'To Julia'...Say, from whom?
Lucetta.   That the contents will show.
Julia.   Say, say...who gave it thee?
Lucetta.   Sir Valentine's page: and sent,
             I think, from Proteus;
He would have given it you, but I, being in the way,   40
Did in your name receive it: pardon the fault, I pray.
 Julia [*feigns anger*]. Now—by my modesty!—a goodly
    broker...
Dare you presume to harbour wanton lines?
To whisper, and conspire against my youth?
Now trust me, 'tis an office of great worth,
And you an officer fit for the place... [*holding out the letter*
There...take the paper...see it be returned,
Or else return no more into my sight.
 Lucetta. To plead for love deserves more fee than hate.
 Julia [*stamps*]. Will you be gone?
 Lucetta [*going within*].   That you may ruminate. 50
 Julia. And yet I would I had o'erlooked the letter;
It were a shame to call her back again,
And pray her to a fault for which I chid her....
What 'fool is she, that knows I am a maid,
And would not force the letter to my view?
Since maids, in modesty, say 'no' to that
Which they would have the profferer construe 'ay'....
Fie, fie! how wayward is this foolish love;
That, like a testy babe, will scratch the nurse,
And presently, all humbled, kiss the rod!   60
How churlishly I chid Lucetta hence,
When willingly I would have had her here!
How angerly I taught my brow to frown,
When inward joy enforced my heart to smile!

My penance is, to call Lucetta back
And ask remission for my folly past....
What ho! Lucetta!

   LUCETTA returning, drops the letter

 Lucetta.   What would your ladyship?
 Julia. Is it near dinner-time?
 Lucetta.   I would it were—
That you might kill your stomach on your meat,
70 And not upon your maid. [*she takes up the letter*
 Julia.   What is't that you
Took up so gingerly?
 Lucetta.   Nothing.
 Julia.   Why didst thou stoop then?
 Lucetta. To take a paper up, that I let fall.
 Julia. And is that paper nothing?
 Lucetta. Nothing concerning me.
 Julia. Then let it lie, for those that it concerns.
 Lucetta. Madam, it will not lie where it concerns,
Unless it have a false interpreter.
 Julia. Some love of yours hath writ to you in rhyme.
 Lucetta. That I might sing it, madam, to a tune...
80 Give me a note—your ladyship can set.
 Julia. As little by such toys as may be possible:
Best sing it to the tune of 'Light o' love.'
 Lucetta. It is too heavy for so light a tune.
 Julia. Heavy? belike it hath some burden then.
 Lucetta. Ay...and melodious were it, would you sing it.
 Julia. And why not you?
 Lucetto.   I cannot reach so high.
 Julia. Let's see your song...

  She snatches at the letter; Lucetta hastily
   hides it behind her back, and runs

     How now, minion! [*giving chase*

Lucetta [*over her shoulder*]. Keep tune there still; so you
    will sing it out...
[*Julia seizes her*] And yet, methinks, I do not like this tune.
 Julia [*pinching her*]. You do not?   90
 Lucetta.   No, madam, 'tis too sharp.
 Julia [*slapping her*]. You—minion—are too saucy.
 Lucetta.   Nay, now you are too flat;
And mar the concord, with too harsh a descant:
There wanteth but a 'mean' to fill your song.
 Julia. The mean is drowned with your unruly bass.
 Lucetta. Indeed, I 'bid the base' for Proteus.
 Julia. This babble shall not henceforth trouble me;
                [*she tears the letter*
Here is a coil with protestation...
Go, get you gone...[*Lucetta stoops*] and let the papers lie... 100
You would be fingring them, to anger me.
 Lucetta. She makes it strange, but she would be
    best pleased
To be so angred with another letter.   [*she goes within*
 Julia. Nay, would I were so angred with the same...
O hateful hands, to tear such loving words;
Injurious wasps, to feed on such sweet honey,
And kill the bees that yield it with your stings;
I'll kiss each several paper, for amends... [*picking up pieces*
Look, here is writ 'kind Julia'...unkind Julia,
As in revenge of thy ingratitude,   110
I throw thy name against the bruising stones,
Trampling contemptuously on thy disdain....
And here is writ 'love-wounded Proteus'....
Poor wounded name: my bosom, as a bed,
Shall lodge thee till thy wound be throughly healed;
And thus I search it with a sovereign kiss....
But twice, or thrice, was 'Proteus' written down...
                [*seeking on her knees*

Be calm, good wind, blow not a word away,
Till I have found each letter in the letter,
120 Except mine own name: that, some whirlwind bear
Unto a ragged, fearful-hanging rock,
And throw it thence into the raging sea....
Lo, here in one line is his name twice writ:
'Poor forlorn Proteus, passionate Proteus:
To the sweet Julia'...that I'll tear away...
And yet I will not, sith so prettily
He couples it to his complaining names;
Thus will I fold them, one upon another;
Now kiss, embrace, contend, do what you will.

LUCETTA returns

130 *Lucetta.* Madam...   [*Julia starts up*
Dinner is ready...and your father stays.
Julia [*coldly*]. Well, let us go.
Lucetta. What, shall these papers lie like tell-tales here?
Julia. If you respect them, best to take them up.
Lucetta. Nay, I was taken up for laying them down....
Yet here they shall not lie, for catching cold.
                          [*she gathers them up*
Julia. I see you have a month's mind to them.
Lucetta. Ay, madam, you may say what sights you see;
I see things too, although you judge I wink.
140 *Julia.* Come, come, will't please you go?
                          [*they go in to dinner*

[1.3.]   *Verona: a room in Antonio's house*

ANTONIO enters with PANTHINO, his man

Antonio. Tell me, Panthino, what sad talk was that,
Wherewith my brother held you in the cloister?
Panthino. 'Twas of his nephew Proteus, your son.

Antonio. Why? what of him?

Panthino.   He wondred that your lordship
Would suffer him to spend his youth at home,
While other men, of slender reputation,
Put forth their sons to seek preferment out:
Some to the wars, to try their fortune there;
Some, to discover islands far away;
Some, to the studious universities..   10
For any or for all these exercises
He said that Proteus, your son, was meet;
And did request me to importune you
To let him spend his time no more at home;
Which would be great impeachment to his age,
In having known no travel in his youth.

Antonio. Nor need'st thou much importune me to that
Whereon this month I have been hammering....
I have considered well his loss of time,
And how he cannot be a perfect man,   20
Not being tried and tutored in the world:
Experience is by industry achieved,
And perfected by the swift course of time:
Then, tell me, whither were I best to send him?

Panthino. I think your lordship is not ignorant,
How his companion, youthful Valentine,
Attends the emperor in his royal court.

Antonio. I know it well.

Panthino. 'Twere good, I think, your lordship sent
     him thither.
There shall he practise tilts and tournaments,   30
Hear sweet discourse, converse with noblemen,
And be in eye of every exercise
Worthy his youth and nobleness of birth.

Antonio. I like thy counsel...well hast thou advised...
And that thou mayst perceive how well I like it,

The execution of it shall make known;
Even with the speediest expedition
I will despatch him to the emperor's court.
   Panthino. To-morrow, may it please you, Don Alphonso,
40 With other gentlemen of good esteem,
Are journeying to salute the emperor,
And to commend their service to his will.
   Antonio. Good company: with them shall Proteus go...

       PROTEUS enters, conning a letter

And in good time...now will we break with him.
   (*Proteus.* Sweet love, sweet lines, sweet life—
Here is her hand, the agent of her heart;
Here is her oath for love, her honour's pawn:
O, that our fathers would applaud our loves,
To seal our happiness with their consents....
50 O heavenly Julia....
   Antonio. How now! what letter are you reading there?
   Proteus. May't please your lordship, 'tis a word or two
Of commendations sent from Valentine;
Delivered by a friend that came from him.
   Antonio. Lend me the letter: let me see what news.
   Proteus. There is no news, my lord, but that he writes
How happily he lives, how well beloved,
And daily gracéd by the emperor;
Wishing me with him, partner of his fortune.
60   *Antonio.* And how stand you affected to his wish?
   Proteus. As one relying on your lordship's will,
And not depending on his friendly wish.
   Antonio. My will is something sorted with his wish:
Muse not that I thus suddenly proceed;
For what I will, I will, and there an end...
I am resolved that thou shalt spend some time
With Valentinus in the emperor's court:

What maintenance he from his friends receives,
Like exhibition thou shalt have from me.
To-morrow be in readiness to go—   70
Excuse it not...for I am péremptory.
  Proteus. My lord, I cannot be so soon provided,
Please you deliberate a day or two.
  Antonio. Look, what thou want'st shall be sent
      after thee:
No more of stay; to-morrow thou must go:
Come on, Panthino; you shall be employed
To hasten on his expedition.
                [*Antonio goes out, followed by Panthino*
  Proteus. Thus have I shunned the fire, for fear of burning,
And drenched me in the sea, where I am drowned....
I feared to show my father Julia's letter,   80
Lest he should take exceptions to my love,
And with the vantage of mine own excuse
Hath he excepted most against my love....
O, how this spring of love resembleth
  The uncertain glory of an April day,
Which now shows all the beauty of the sun,
  And by and by a cloud takes all away.

                PANTHINO comes to the door

  Panthino. Sir Proteus, your father calls for you—
He is in haste, therefore I pray you go.
  Proteus. Why, this it is: my heart accords thereto,   90
And yet a thousand times it answers 'no.'   [*he goes out*

[2.1.]   *A street in Milan*
      VALENTINE with SPEED following: VALENTINE
                drops a glove
  Speed [*runs up*]. Sir, your glove.
  Valentine. Not mine: my gloves are on.

Speed. Why then this may be yours, for this is but one.

Valentine. Ha! let me see...ay, give it me, it's mine...
Sweet ornament that decks a thing divine—
Ah Silvia, Silvia.

Speed [*calls*]. Madam Silvia! Madam Silvia!

Valentine. How now, sirrah!

Speed. She is not within hearing, sir.

10 *Valentine.* Why, sir, who bade you call her?

Speed. Your worship, sir, or else I mistook.

Valentine. Well: you'll still be too forward.

Speed. And yet I was last chidden for being too slow.

Valentine. Go to, sir, tell me: do you know Madam Silvia?

Speed. She that your worship loves?

Valentine. Why, how know you that I am in love?

Speed. Marry, by these special marks: first, you have
learned—like Sir Proteus—to wreath your arms like a
malcontent; to relish a love-song, like a robin-redbreast;
20 to walk alone, like one that had the pestilence; to sigh,
like a school-boy that had lost his A. B. C; to weep, like
a young wench that had buried her grandam; to fast, like
one that takes diet; to watch, like one that fears robbing;
to speak puling, like a beggar at Hallowmas...You were
wont, when you laughed, to crow like a cock; when you
walked, to walk like one of the lions; when you fasted, it
was presently after dinner; when you looked sadly, it was
for want of money: and now you are metamorphosed with
a mistress, that, when I look on you, I can hardly think
30 you my master.

Valentine. Are all these things perceived in me?

Speed. They are all perceived without ye.

Valentine. Without me? they cannot.

Speed. Without you? nay, that's certain; for, without
you were so simple, none else would: but you are so
without these follies, that these follies are within you,

and shine through you like the water in an urinal: that not an eye that sees you, but is a physician to comment on your malady.

Valentine. But tell me: dost thou know my Lady Silvia? 40

Speed. She that you gaze on so, as she sits at supper?

Valentine. Hast thou observed that? even she I mean.

Speed. Why sir, I know her not.

Valentine. Dost thou know her by my gazing on her, and yet know'st her not?

Speed. Is she not hard-favoured, sir?

Valentine. Not so fair, boy, as well-favoured.

Speed. Sir, I know that well enough.

Valentine. What dost thou know?

Speed. That she is not so fair, as (of you) well-favoured. 50

Valentine. I mean that her beauty is exquisite, but her favour infinite.

Speed. That's because the one is painted, and the other out of all count.

Valentine. How painted? and how out of count?

Speed. Marry, sir, so painted, to make her fair, that no man counts of her beauty.

Valentine. How esteem'st thou me? I account of her beauty.

Speed. You never saw her since she was deformed. 60

Valentine. How long hath she been deformed?

Speed. Ever since you loved her.

Valentine. I have loved her ever since I saw her, and still I see her beautiful.

Speed. If you love her, you cannot see her.

Valentine. Why?

Speed. Because love is blind...O, that you had mine eyes, or your own eyes had the lights they were wont to have, when you chid at Sir Proteus for going ungartered.

Valentine. What should I see then? 70

Speed. Your own present folly, and her passing de-
formity: for he, being in love, could not see to garter his
hose; and you, being in love, cannot see to put on your
hose.

Valentine. Belike, boy, then you are in love—for last
morning you could not see to wipe my shoes.

Speed. True, sir: I was in love with my bed. I thank you,
you swinged me for my love, which makes me the bolder
to chide you for yours.

80 *Valentine.* In conclusion, I stand affected to her.

Speed. I would you were set, so your affection would
cease.

Valentine. Last night she enjoined me to write some lines
to one she loves.

Speed. And have you?

Valentine. I have.

Speed. Are they not lamely writ?

Valentine. No, boy, but as well as I can do them...
Peace, here she comes.

SILVIA approaches with her maid

90 (*Speed.* O excellent motion...O exceeding puppet...now
will he interpret to her.

Valentine [*bows low*]. Madam and mistress, a thousand
good-morrows.

(*Speed.* O, 'give-ye-good-e'en...here's a million of
manners!

Silvia [*bows*]. Sir Valentine and servant, to you two
thousand.

(*Speed.* He should give her interest: and she gives it him.

Valentine. As you enjoined me; I have writ your letter
100 Unto the secret nameless friend of yours...

                         [*he gives it her*

Which I was much unwilling to proceed in,

But for my duty to your ladyship.

  Silvia [*perusing it*]. I thank you, gentle servant—'tis very
    clerkly done.

  Valentine. Now trust me, madam, it came hardly off:
For, being ignorant to whom it goes,
I writ at random, very doubtfully.

  Silvia [*coldly*]. Perchance you think too much of so
    much pains?

  Valentine. No, madam, so it stead you, I will write—
Please you command—a thousand times as much...
And yet—   110

  Silvia. A pretty period...well...I guess the sequel;
'And yet I will not name it': 'and yet I care not'....

                              [*she offers him the letter*
And yet take this again: and yet I thank you:
Meaning henceforth to trouble you no more.

  (*Speed*. And yet you will: and yet another 'yet.'

  Valentine [*flushing*]. What means your ladyship?
    Do you not like it?

  Silvia. Yes, yes: the lines are very quaintly writ,
But—since unwillingly—take them again....

                              [*offering the letter again*
Nay, take them.

  Valentine.   Madam, they are for you.

  Silvia. Ay, ay: you writ them, sir, at my request,   120
But I will none of them: they are for you:
I would have had them writ more movingly...

                              [*he takes the letter*

  Valentine. Please you, I'll write your ladyship another.

  Silvia. And when it's writ...for my sake read it over,
And, if it please you, so...if not...why, so...

  Valentine. If it please me, madam, what then?

  Silvia. Why, if it please you, take it for your labour;
And so good-morrow, servant.   [*she bows and passes on*

Speed. O jest unseen...inscrutable...invisible,

130 As a nose on a man's face, or a weathercock on a steeple...
My master sues to her: and she hath taught her suitor,
He being her pupil, to become her tutor....
O excellent device! was there ever heard a better?
That my master, being scribe, to himself should write
    the letter?

Valentine. How now, sir! what are you reasoning with
yourself?

Speed. Nay...I was rhyming...'tis you that have the
reason.

Valentine. To do what?

140 *Speed.* To be a spokesman from Madam Silvia.

Valentine. To whom?

Speed. To yourself...why, she wooes you by a figure.

Valentine. What figure?

Speed. By a letter, I should say.

Valentine. Why, she hath not writ to me?

Speed. What need she, when she hath made you write
to yourself? Why, do you not perceive the jest?

Valentine. No, believe me.

Speed. No believing you indeed, sir:

150 But did you perceive her earnest?

Valentine. She gave me none, except an angry word.

Speed. Why, she hath given you a letter.

Valentine. That's the letter I writ to her friend.

Speed. And that letter hath she delivered, and there
    an end.

Valentine. I would it were no worse.

Speed. I'll warrant you, 'tis as well:

For often you have writ to her: and she, in modesty,
Or else for want of idle time, could not again reply—
Or fearing else some messenger, that might her
    mind discover,

Herself hath taught her love himself to write unto
   her lover!   160
All this I speak in print, for in print I found it....
Why muse you, sir? 'tis dinner-time.
  Valentine [*sighs*]. I have dined.
  Speed. Ay, but hearken, sir: though the chameleon Love
can feed on the air, I am one that am nourished by my
victuals; and would fain have meat: O, be not like your
mistress—be moved, be moved.   [*they move on*

[2.2.]   *Verona: the street near Julia's house*
    PROTEUS *and* JULIA *on a seat beneath the trees*

  Proteus. Have patience, gentle Julia...
  Julia. I must, where is no remedy.
  Proteus. When possibly I can, I will return.
  Julia. If you turn not...you will return the sooner:
Keep this remembrance for thy Julia's sake.
             [*she gives him a ring*
  Proteus. Why then we'll make exchange; here, take
  you this.   [*he gives her another*
  Julia. And seal the bargain with a holy kiss.
  Proteus. Here is my hand for my true constancy...
And when that hour o'er-slips me in the day,
Wherein I sigh not, Julia, for thy sake,   10
The next ensuing hour some foul mischance
Torment me for my love's forgetfulness...
My father stays my coming...answer not...
The tide is now; nay, not thy tide of tears—
That tide will stay me longer than I should....
Julia, farewell... [*they embrace; she goes within, weeping*
        What! gone without a word?
Ay, so true love should do: it cannot speak—
For truth hath better deeds than words to grace it.

PANTHINO appears in the distance

Panthino [*calling*]. Sir Proteus! you are stayed for.
Proteus.   Go...I come, I come...
20 Alas, this parting strikes poor lovers dumb.   [*he goes*

[2.3.] *LAUNCE slowly approaches weeping, leading a dog,*
which he ties to a tree

Launce. Nay, 'twill be this hour ere I have done weeping:
all the kind of the Launces have this very fault...I have
received my proportion, like the Prodigious Son, and am
going with Sir Proteus to the Imperial's court...I think
Crab, my dog, be the sourest-natured dog that lives: my
mother weeping; my father wailing; my sister crying; our
maid howling; our cat wringing her hands; and all our
house in a great perplexity—yet did not this cruel-hearted
cur shed one tear: he is a stone, a very pebble-stone, and
10 has no more pity in him than a dog: a Jew would have
wept to have seen our parting: why, my grandam having
no eyes, look you, wept herself blind at my parting: nay,
I'll show you the manner of it.... [*takes off his shoes*]
This shoe is my father...no, this left shoe is my father;
no, no, this left shoe is my mother...nay, that cannot be
so neither...yes; it is so, it is so: it hath the worser sole...
this shoe, with the hole in it, is my mother, and this my
father...a vengeance on't! there 'tis...[*places them on the*
seat]. Now, sir, this staff is my sister; for, look you, she is
20 as white as a lily, and as small as a wand: this hat is Nan,
our maid: I am the dog...no, the dog is himself, and I am
the dog...O, the dog is me, and I am myself: ay; so, so...
Now come I to my father; [*kneels*] 'Father, your blessing':
now should not the shoe speak a word for weeping: now
should I kiss my father; [*kisses one shoe*] well, he weeps
on...Now come I to my mother: O, that she could speak

now, like a †wood woman: well, I kiss her: [*kisses the other shoe*] why there 'tis; here's my mother's breath up and down...Now come I to my sister; mark the moan she makes...now the dog all this while sheds not a tear; nor 30 speaks a word: but see how I lay the dust with my tears.

PANTHINO returns, in haste

Panthino. Launce, away, away...aboard...thy master is shipped, and thou art to post after with oars...What's the matter? why weep'st thou, man? Away ass, you'll lose the tide, if you tarry any longer.

Launce [*sorrowfully*]. It is no matter if the tied were lost, for it is the unkindest tied that ever any man tied.

Panthino. What's the unkindest tide?

Launce. Why, he that's tied here, Crab, my dog.

Panthino. Tut, man: I mean thou'lt lose the flood, and 40 in losing the flood lose thy voyage, and in losing thy voyage lose thy master, and in losing thy master lose thy service, and in losing thy service—why dost thou stop my mouth?

Launce. For fear thou shouldst lose thy tongue.

Panthino. Where should I lose my tongue?

Launce. In thy tale.

Panthino. In my tail!

Launce. Lose the tide, and the voyage, and the master, and the service—and the tied...[*he looses Crab*] Why, 50 man, if the river were dry, I am able to fill it with my tears; if the wind were down, I could drive the boat with my sighs.

Panthino. Come: come away, man—I was sent to call thee.

Launce [*threatening*]. Sir...call me what thou dar'st!

Panthino. Wilt thou go?

Launce. Well, I will go.   [*they hurry away*

[2.4.]   *Milan: a room in the Duke's palace*

VALENTINE *and* SILVIA, *seated together, talking in low
tones;* SPEED *behind* VALENTINE; *Sir* THURIO (*foppishly
attired*) *watching them at a distance*

Silvia. Servant.

Valentine. Mistress!

Speed [in his ear]. Master, Sir Thurio frowns on you.

Valentine. Ay, boy, it's for love.

Speed. Not of you.

Valentine. Of my mistress then.

Speed. 'Twere good you knocked him.   [*he goes out*

Silvia [lightly, aloud] Servant, you are sad.

Valentine. Indeed, madam, I seem so.

10 *Thurio.* Seem you that you are not?

Valentine. Haply I do.

Thurio. So do counterfeits.

Valentine. So do you.

Thurio. What seem I that I am not?

Valentine. Wise.

Thurio. What instance of the contrary?

Valentine. Your folly.

Thurio. And how quote you my folly?

Valentine. I quote it in your jerkin.

20 *Thurio.* My jerkin is a doublet.

Valentine. Well, then, I'll double your folly.

Thurio. How!

Silvia. What, angry, Sir Thurio? do you change colour?

Valentine. Give him leave, madam—he is a kind of
chameleon.

Thurio. That hath more mind to feed on your blood,
than live in your air.

Valentine. You have said, sir.

Thurio. Ay, sir, and done too, for this time.

Valentine. I know it well, sir, you always end ere you 30
begin.

Silvia. A fine volley of words, gentlemen, and quickly
shot off.

Valentine. 'Tis indeed, madam—we thank the giver.

Silvia. Who is that, servant?

Valentine. Yourself, sweet lady, for you gave the fire.
Sir Thurio borrows his wit from your ladyship's looks,
and spends what he borrows, kindly in your company.

Thurio. Sir, if you spend word for word with me, I shall
make your wit bankrupt.   40

Valentine. I know it well, sir: you have an exchequer of
words, and, I think, no other treasure to give your fol-
lowers: for it appears by their bare liveries, that they
live by your bare words.

Silvia. No more, gentlemen, no more...Here comes my
father.

The DUKE enters with a letter in his hand

Duke [*smiling*]. Now, daughter Silvia, you are
          hard beset....
Sir Valentine, your father is in good health—
What say you to a letter from your friends
Of much good news?

Valentine.   My lord, I will be thankful   50
To any happy messenger from thence.

Duke. Know you Don Antonio, your countryman?

Valentine. Ay, my good lord, I know the gentleman
To be of worth, and worthy estimation,
And not without desert so well reputed.

Duke. Hath he not a son?

Valentine. Ay, my good lord—a son that well deserves
The honour and regard of such a father.

Duke. You know him well?

60 *Valentine.* I know him as myself: for from our infancy
We have conversed, and spent our hours together,
And though myself have been an idle truant,
Omitting the sweet benefit of time
To clothe mine age with angel-like perfection...
Yet hath Sir Proteus, for that's his name,
Made use and fair advantage of his days:
His years but young, but his experience old:
His head unmellowed, but his judgement ripe:
And, in a word, (for far behind his worth
70 Come all the praises that I now bestow)
He is complete in feature and in mind,
With all good grace, to grace a gentleman.
  Duke. Beshrew me, sir, but if he make this good,
He is as worthy for an empress' love,
As meet to be an emperor's counsellor...
Well, sir: this gentleman is come to me
With commendation from great potentates,
And here he means to spend his time awhile.
I think 'tis no unwelcome news to you.
80 *Valentine.* Should I have wished a thing, it had been he.
  Duke. Welcome him then according to his worth:
Silvia, I speak to you, and you, Sir Thurio—
For Valentine, I need not cite him to it.
I will send him hither to you presently.   [*he goes out*
  Valentine. This is the gentleman I told your ladyship
Had come along with me, but that his mistress
Did hold his eyes locked in her crystal looks.
  Silvia. Belike that now she hath enfranchised them
Upon some other pawn for fealty.
90 *Valentine.* Nay, sure, I think she holds them prisoners still.
  Silvia. Nay, then he should be blind—and, being blind,
How could he see his way to seek out you?
  Valentine. Why, lady, love hath twenty pair of eyes.

Thurio. They say that Love hath not an eye at all.
Valentine. To see such lovers, Thurio, as yourself—
Upon a homely object love can wink.
Silvia. Have done, have done: here comes the gentleman.

> PROTEUS *enters;* THURIO *goes out, shrugging*
> *his shoulders*

Valentine. Welcome, dear Proteus...[*they embrace*] Mis-
       tress, I beseech you,
Confirm his welcome with some special favour.
Silvia. His worth is warrant for his welcome hither,   100
If this be he you oft have wished to hear from.
Valentine. Mistress, it is...[*he presents him*] Sweet lady,
       entertain him
To be my fellow-servant to your ladyship.
Silvia [*bowing*]. Too low a mistress for so high a servant.
Proteus. Not so, sweet lady, but too mean a servant
To have a look of such a worthy mistress.
Valentine. Leave off discourse of disability...
Sweet lady, entertain him for your servant.
Proteus. My duty will I boast of, nothing else.
Silvia. And duty never yet did want his meed....   110
                                   [*he kisses her hand*
Servant, you are welcome to a worthless mistress.
Proteus. I'll die on him that says so, but yourself.
Silvia. That you are welcome?
Proteus.   That you are worthless.

> THURIO *returns*

Thurio. Madam, my lord your father would speak
       with you.
Silvia. I wait upon his pleasure...Come, Sir Thurio,
Go with me...Once more, new servant, welcome;
I'll leave you to confer of home-affairs.
When you have done, we look to hear from you.

Proteus. We'll both attend upon your ladyship.

                        [*Silvia goes out, with Thurio*

120 *Valentine.* Now tell me: how do all from whence you came?

Proteus. Your friends are well, and have them much

    commended.

Valentine. And how do yours?

Proteus.   I left them all in health.

Valentine. How does your lady? and how thrives your love?

Proteus. My tales of love were wont to weary you,

I know you joy not in a love-discourse.

Valentine. Ay, Proteus, but that life is altered now.

I have done penance for contemning Love,

Whose high imperious thoughts have punished me

With bitter fasts, with penitential groans,

130 With nightly tears, and daily heart-sore sighs,

For, in revenge of my contempt of love,

Love hath chased sleep from my enthrallèd eyes,

And made them watchers of mine own heart's sorrow....

O, gentle Proteus, Love's a mighty lord,

And hath so humbled me, as I confess

There is no woe to his correction,

Nor to his service no such joy on earth:

Now, no discourse, except it be of love:

Now can I break my fast, dine, sup, and sleep,

140 Upon the very naked name of love.

Proteus. Enough; I read your fortune in your eye:

Was this the idol that you worship so?

Valentine. Even she; and is she not a heavenly saint?

Proteus. No; but she is an earthly paragon.

Valentine. Call her divine.

Proteus.   I will not flatter her.

Valentine. O, flatter me; for love delights in praises.

Proteus. When I was sick, you gave me bitter pills,

And I must minister the like to you.

Valentine. Then speak the truth by her; if not divine,
Yet let her be a principality,   150
Sovereign to all the creatures on the earth.

  Proteus. Except my mistress.

  Valentine.   Sweet: except not any,
Except thou wilt except against my love.

  Proteus. Have I not reason to prefer mine own?

  Valentine. And I will help thee to prefer her too:
She shall be dignified with this high honour—
To bear my lady's train, lest the base earth
Should from her vesture chance to steal a kiss,
And, of so great a favour growing proud,
Disdain to root the summer-swelling flower,   160
And make rough winter everlastingly.

  Proteus. Why, Valentine, what braggardism is this?

  Valentine. Pardon me, Proteus, all I can is nothing
To her, whose worth makes other worthies nothing;
She is alone.

  Proteus.   Then let her alone.

  Valentine. Not for the world: why man, she is mine own,
And I as rich in having such a jewel
As twenty seas, if all their sand were pearl,
The water nectar, and the rocks pure gold....
Forgive me that I do not dream on thee,   170
Because thou seest me dote upon my love:
My foolish rival, that her father likes—
Only for his possessions are so huge—
Is gone with her along, and I must after,
For love, thou know'st, is full of jealousy.

  Proteus. But she loves you?

  Valentine. Ay, and we are betrothed: nay more, our
        marriage hour,
With all the cunning manner of our flight,
Determined of: how I must climb her window—

180 The ladder made of cords—and all the means
Plotted and 'greed on for my happiness....
Good Proteus, go with me to my chamber,
In these affairs to aid me with thy counsel.
  Proteus. Go on before: I shall enquire you forth:
I must unto the road, to disembark
Some necessaries that I needs must use,
And then I'll presently attend you.
  Valentine [*at the door*]. Will you make haste?
  Proteus. I will....   [*Valentine departs*
190 Even as one heat another heat expels,
Or as one nail by strength drives out another,
So the remembrance of my former love
Is by a newer object quite forgotten.
†It is mine....or Valentine's praise,
Her true perfection, or my false transgression,
That makes me, reasonless, to reason thus?
She is fair; and so is Julia that I love—
That I did love, for now my love is thawed,
Which, like a waxen image 'gainst a fire,
200 Bears no impression of the thing it was....
Methinks my zeal to Valentine is cold,
And that I love him not as I was wont:
O, but I love his lady too-too much,
And that's the reason I love him so little....
How shall I dote on her with more advice,
That thus without advice begin to love her?
'Tis but her picture I have yet beheld,
And that hath dazzléd my reason's light:
But when I look on her perfections,
210 There is no reason but I shall be blind....
If I can check my erring love, I will—
If not, to compass her I'll use my skill.
                              [*he goes out, musing*

[2.5.]   *Milan: a street near the quay;*
an alehouse hard by

SPEED *meeting* LAUNCE *and his dog*

Speed. Launce! by mine honesty, welcome to †Padua.

Launce. Forswear not thyself, sweet youth, for I am not welcome....I reckon this always—that a man is never undone till he be hanged, nor never welcome to a place till some certain shot be paid and the hostess say 'welcome.'

Speed. Come on, you madcap: I'll to the alehouse with you presently; where, for one shot of five pence, thou shalt have five thousand welcomes...But, sirrah, how did thy master part with Madam Julia?

Launce. Marry, after they closed in earnest, they parted 10 very fairly in jest.

Speed. But shall she marry him?

Launce. No.

Speed. How then? Shall he marry her?

Launce. No, neither.

Speed. What, are they broken?

Launce. No; they are both as whole as a fish.

Speed. Why then, how stands the matter with them?

Launce. Marry, thus—when it stands well with him, it stands well with her.   20

Speed. What an ass art thou! I understand thee not.

Launce. What a block art thou, that thou canst not! My staff understands me!

Speed. What thou sayst?

Launce. Ay, and what I do too: look thee, I'll but lean, and my staff understands me.

Speed. It stands under thee, indeed.

Launce. Why, stand under...and understand is all one.

Speed. But tell me true, will't be a match?

30 *Launce.* Ask my dog—if he say 'ay,' it will: if he say 'no,' it will: if he shake his tail and say nothing, it will.

Speed. The conclusion is then, that it will.

Launce. Thou shalt never get such a secret from me, but by a parable.

Speed. 'Tis well that I get it so...But Launce, how sayst thou, that my master is become a notable lover?

Launce. I never knew him otherwise.

Speed. Than how?

Launce. A notable lubber: as thou reportest him to be.

40 *Speed.* Why, thou whoreson ass, thou mistak'st me.

Launce. Why, fool, I meant not thee, I meant thy master.

Speed. I tell thee, my master is become a hot lover.

Launce. Why, I tell thee, I care not though he burn himself in love....If thou wilt, go with me to the alehouse; if not, thou art an Hebrew, a Jew, and not worth the name of a Christian.

Speed. Why?

Launce. Because thou hast not so much charity in thee, as to 'go to the ale' with a Christian...Wilt thou go?

50 *Speed.* At thy service.   [*they enter the alehouse*

[2.6.]   *PROTEUS slowly passes, on his way
                  to the quay*

Proteus. To leave my Julia...shall I be forsworn?
To love fair Silvia...shall I be forsworn?
To wrong my friend, I shall be much forsworn....
And e'en that power, which gave me first my oath,
Provokes me to this threefold perjury....
Love bade me swear, and love bids me forswear;
O sweet-suggesting Love, if thou has sinned,
Teach me—thy tempted subject—to excuse it....
At first I did adore a twinkling star,
10 But now I worship a celestial sun:

Unheedful vows may heedfully be broken,
And he wants wit that wants resolvéd will
To learn his wit t'exchange the bad for better;
Fie, fie, unreverend tongue, to call her bad,
Whose sovereignty so oft thou hast preferred
With twenty thousand soul-confirming oaths....
I cannot leave to love; and yet I do:
But there I leave to love where I should lóve....
Julia I lose, and Valentine I lose—
If I keep them, I needs must lose myself: 20
If I lose them, thus find I by their loss—
For Valentine, myself: for Julia, Silvia....
I to myself am dearer than a friend,
For love is still more precious in itself:
And Silvia—witness Heaven, that made her fair!—
Shews Julia but a swarthy Ethiop....
I will forget that Julia is alive,
Remembring that my love to her is dead....
And Valentine I'll hold an enemy,
Aiming at Silvia as a sweeter friend....   30
I cannot now prove constant to myself,
Without some treachery used to Valentine....
This night he meaneth with a corded ladder
To climb celestial Silvia's chamber-window,
Myself in counsel his competitor....
Now presently I'll give her father notice
Of their disguising and pretended flight:
Who, all enraged, will banish Valentine:
For Thurio he intends shall wed his daughter.   40
But, Valentine being gone, I'll quickly cross
By some sly trick blunt Thurio's dull proceeding....
Love, lend me wings to make my purpose swift,
As thou hast lent me wit to plot this drift!

                                [he continues his way

[2.7.]   *Verona: a room in Julia's house*

        JULIA, studying a map; LUCETTA, sewing

Julia [*looks up*]. Counsel, Lucetta, gentle girl assist me.
And, e'en in kind love, I do cónjure thee,
Who art the table wherein all my thoughts
Are visibly charáctered and engraved,
To lesson me, and tell me some good mean,
How, with my honour, I may undertake
A journey to my loving Proteus.
        Lucetta. Alas, the way is wearisome and long.
        Julia. A true-devoted pilgrim is not weary
10 To measure kingdoms with his feeble steps—
Much less shall she that hath Love's wings to fly,
And when the flight is made to one so dear,
Of such divine perfection, as Sir Proteus.
        Lucetta. Better forbear till Proteus make return.
        Julia. O, know'st thou not his looks are my soul's food?
Pity the dearth that I have pinéd in,
By longing for that food so long a time....
Didst thou but know the inly touch of love,
Thou wouldst as soon go kindle fire with snow,
20 As seek to quench the fire of love with words.
        Lucetta. I do not seek to quench your love's hot fire,
But qualify the fire's éxtreme rage,
Lest it should burn above the bounds of reason.
        Julia. The more thou damm'st it up, the more it burns:
The current that with gentle murmur glides,
Thou know'st, being stopped, impatiently doth rage:
But when his fair course is not hinderéd
He makes sweet music with th'enamelled stones,
Giving a gentle kiss to every sedge
30 He overtaketh in his pilgrimage;
And so by many winding nooks he strays,

With willing sport, to the wild ocean....
Then let me go, and hinder not my course:
I'll be as patient as a gentle stream,
And make a pastime of each weary step,
Till the last step have brought me to my love—
And there I'll rest, as after much turmoil
A blessèd soul doth in Elysium.

 Lucetta. But in what habit will you go along?

 Julia. Not like a woman, for I would prevent 40
The loose encounters of lascivious men:
Gentle Lucetta, fit me with such weeds
As may beseem some well-reputed page.

 Lucetta. Why then your ladyship must cut your hair.

 Julia. No, girl, I'll knit it up in silken strings,
With twenty odd-conceited true-love knots:
To be fantastic may become a youth
Of greater time than I shall show to be.

 Lucetta. What fashion—madam—shall I make
  your breeches?

 Julia. That fits as well as 'Tell me, good my lord, 50
What compass will you wear your farthingale?'
Why, e'en what fashion thou best likes, Lucetta.

 Lucetta. You must needs have them with a cod-
  piece, madam.

 Julia. Out, out, Lucetta! that will be ill-favoured.

 Lucetta. A round hose, madam, now's not worth a pin,
Unless you have a cod-piece to stick pins on.

 Julia. Lucetta, as thou lov'st me, let me have
What thou think'st meet, and is most mannerly....
But tell me, wench, how will the world repute me
For undertaking so unstaid a journey? 60
I fear me, it will make me scandalized.

 Lucetta. If you think so, then stay at home and go not.

 Julia. Nay, that I will not.

Lucetta. Then never dream on infamy, but go:
If Proteus like your journey when you come,
No matter who's displeased when you are gone:
I fear me, he will scarce be pleased with all.
Julia. That is the least, Lucetta, of my fear:
A thousand oaths, an ocean of his tears,
70 And instances of infinite of love,
Warrant me welcome to my Proteus.
Lucetta. All these are servants to deceitful men.
Julia. Base men, that use them to so base effect;
But truer stars did govern Proteus' birth—
His words are bonds, his oaths are oracles,
His love sincere, his thoughts immaculate,
His tears pure messengers sent from his heart,
His heart as far from fraud as heaven from earth.
Lucetta. Pray heaven he prove so, when you come to him.
80 *Julia.* Now, as thou lov'st me, do him not that wrong
To bear a hard opinion of his truth:
Only deserve my love by loving him,
And presently go with me to my chamber,
To take a note of what I stand in need of
To furnish me upon my longing journey:
All that is mine I leave at thy dispose,
My goods, my lands, my reputation,
Only, in lieu thereof, dispatch me hence:
Come; answer not: but to it presently—
90 I am impatient of my tarriance.   [*they go out*

[3.1.]   *Milan: before the Duke's palace*

The DUKE, *THURIO and* PROTEUS *come forth*

Duke. Sir Thurio, give us leave, I pray, awhile—
We have some secrets to confer about....

[*Thurio bows and departs*

Now, tell me, Proteus, what's your will with me?
  Proteus. My gracious lord, that which I would discover
The law of friendship bids me to conceal,
But when I call to mind your gracious favours
Done to me—undeserving as I am—
My duty pricks me on to utter that
Which else no worldly good should draw from me:
Know, worthy prince, Sir Valentine, my friend,   10
This night intends to steal away your daughter:
Myself am one made privy to the plot....
I know you have determined to bestow her
On Thurio, whom your gentle daughter hates,
And should she thus be stol'n away from you,
It would be much vexation to your age....
Thus—for my duty's sake—I rather chose
To cross my friend in his intended drift,
Than, by concealing it, heap on your head
A pack of sorrows which would press you down,   20
Being unprevented, to your timeless grave.
  Duke. Proteus, I thank thee for thine honest care,
Which to requite, command me while I live....
This love of theirs myself have often seen,
Haply when they have judged me fast asleep,
And oftentimes have purposed to forbid
Sir Valentine her company and my court:
But, fearing lest my jealous aim might err,
And so, unworthily, disgrace the man—
A rashness that I ever yet have shunned—   30
I gave him gentle looks, thereby to find
That which thyself hast now disclosed to me....
And, that thou mayst perceive my fear of this,
Knowing that tender youth is soon suggested,
I nightly lodge her in an upper tower,
The key whereof myself have ever kept:

And thence she cannot be conveyed away.

Proteus. Know, noble lord, they have devised a mean
How he her chamber-window will ascend,
40 And with a corded ladder fetch her down:
For which the youthful lover now is gone,
And this way comes he with it presently;
Where, if it please you, you may intercept him....
But, good my lord, do it so cunningly,
That my discovery be not aiméd at:
For love of you, not hate unto my friend,
Hath made me publisher of this pretence.

Duke. Upon mine honour, he shall never know
That I had any light from thee of this.

50 *Proteus.* Adieu, my lord, Sir Valentine is coming.

　　　　　　　　　　　　　　[he retires into the palace
　　　VALENTINE *passes hurriedly, cloaked and booted*

Duke. Sir Valentine, whither away so fast?

Valentine. Please it your grace, there is a messenger
That stays to bear my letters to my friends,
And I am going to deliver them.

Duke. Be they of much import?

Valentine. The tenour of them doth but signify
My health and happy being at your court.

Duke. Nay then, no matter: stay with me awhile—
I am to break with thee of some affairs
60 That touch me near: wherein thou must be secret....

　　　　　　　　　　　　　　[he takes him by the arm
'Tis not unknown to thee, that I have sought
To match my friend Sir Thurio to my daughter.

Valentine. I know it well, my lord—and, sure, the match
Were rich and honourable: besides, the gentleman
Is full of virtue, bounty, worth, and qualities
Beseeming such a wife as your fair daughter:
Cannot your grace win her to fancy him?

Duke. No, trust me, she is peevish, sullen, froward,
Proud, disobedient, stubborn, lacking duty,
Neither regarding that she is my child,   70
Nor fearing me as if I were her father:
And, may I say to thee, this pride of hers—
Upon advice—hath drawn my love from her,
And where I thought the remnant of mine age
Should have been cherished by her child-like duty,
I now am full resolved to take a wife,
And turn her out to who will take her in:
Then let her beauty be her wedding-dower:
For me, and my possessions, she esteems not.
  Valentine. What would your grace have me to do in this? 80
  Duke. There is a lady in †Verona here
Whom I affect: but she is nice and coy,
And nought esteems my agéd eloquence....
Now, therefore, would I have thee to my tutor—
For long agone I have forgot to court,
Besides, the fashion of the time is changed—
How and which way I may bestow myself
To be regarded in her sun-bright eye.
  Valentine. Win her with gifts, if she respect not words.
Dumb jewels often, in their silent kind,   90
More than quick words do move a woman's mind.
  Duke. But she did scorn a present that I sent her.
  Valentine. A woman sometime scorns what best
        contents her....
Send her another: never give her o'er—
For scorn at first makes after-love the more:
If she do frown, 'tis not in hate of you,
But rather to beget more love in you:
If she do chide, 'tis not to have you gone,
For why, the fools are mad, if left alone:
Take no repulse, whatever she doth say—   100

For 'get you gone' she doth not mean 'away':
Flatter and praise, commend, extol their graces:
Though ne'er so black, say they have angels' faces.
That man that hath a tongue, I say, is no man,
If with his tongue he cannot win a woman.

　　Duke. But she I mean is promised by her friends
Unto a youthful gentleman of worth,
And kept severely from resort of men,
That no man hath access by day to her.

110　*Valentine.* Why, then, I would resort to her by night.

　　Duke. Ay, but the doors be locked and keys kept safe,
That no man hath recourse to her by night.

　　Valentine. What lets but one may enter at her window?

　　Duke. Her chamber is aloft, far from the ground,
And built so shelving, that one cannot climb it
Without apparent hazard of his life.

　　Valentine. Why, then, a ladder quaintly made of cords,
To cast up, with a pair of anchoring hooks,
Would serve to scale another Hero's tower,

120 So bold Leander would adventure it.

　　Duke. Now, as thou art a gentleman of blood,
Advise me where I may have such a ladder.

　　Valentine. When would you use it? pray sir, tell me that.

　　Duke. This very night; for Love is like a child,
That longs for every thing that he can come by.

　　Valentine. By seven o'clock I'll get you such a ladder.

　　Duke. But, hark thee: I will go to her alone—
How shall I best convey the ladder thither?

　　Valentine. It will be light, my lord, that you may bear it

130 Under a cloak that is of any length.

　　Duke. A cloak as long as thine will serve the turn?

　　Valentine. Ay, my good lord.

　　Duke. 　　　　　　　　　Then let me see thy cloak—
I'll get me one of such another length.

Valentine. Why, any cloak will serve the turn, my lord.
Duke. How shall I fashion me to wear a cloak?
I pray thee, let me feel thy cloak upon me....

    He snatches Valentine's cloak; the ladder
       and a letter fall to the ground

What letter is this same? What's here?—'To Silvia'?
And here an engine fit for my proceeding!
I'll be so bold to break the seal for once.   *[he reads*

  'My thoughts do harbour with my Silvia nightly,   140
  'And slaves they are to me, that send them flying.
  'O, could their master come, and go as lightly,
  'Himself would lodge, where—senseless—they are lying.

  'My herald thoughts in thy pure bosom rest them,
  'While I, their king, that thither them importune,
  'Do curse the grace that with such grace hath
      blessed them,
  'Because myself do want my servants' fortune.

  'I curse myself, for they are sent by me,
  'That they should harbour where their lord should be.'
What's here?   150
  'Silvia, this night I will enfranchise thee'....
'Tis so: and here's the ladder for the purpose....
                [he turns on Valentine
Why, Phaethon—for thou art Merops' son!—
Wilt thou aspire to guide the heavenly car,
And with thy daring folly burn the world?
Wilt thou reach stars, because they shine on thee?
Go base intruder, over-weening slave,
Bestow thy fawning smiles on equal mates,
And think my patience, more than thy desert,
Is privilege for thy departure hence....   160
Thank me for this more than for all the favours,
Which—all too much!—I have bestowed on thee....

But if thou linger in my territories
Longer than swiftest expedition
Will give thee time to leave our royal court,
By heaven, my wrath shall far exceed the love
I ever bore my daughter, or thyself....

        [Valentine throws himself at his feet

Be gone, I will not hear thy vain excuse,
But, as thou lov'st thy life, make speed from hence.

      [he turns upon his heel and goes into the palace

170 *Valentine [prostrate].* And why not death, rather than
    living torment?
To die, is to be banished from myself,
And Silvia is myself: banished from her,
†Is self from self....Ah! deadly banishment:
What light is light, if Silvia be not seen?
What joy is joy, if Silvia be not by?
Unless it be to think that she is by,
And feed upon the shadow of perfection....
Except I be by Silvia in the night,
There is no music in the nightingale....
180 Unless I look on Silvia in the day,
There is no day for me to look upon....
She is my essence—and I leave to be,
If I be not by her fair influence
Fostered, illumined, cherished, kept alive....
I fly not death, to fly his deadly doom—
Tarry I here, I but attend on death—
But, fly I hence, I fly away from life.

        [he buries his face on the ground

    PROTEUS *and* LAUNCE *come from the palace*

Proteus. Run, boy, run, run, and seek him out.
Launce [courses up and down, and then halloos]. So-ho!
    so-ho!
Proteus. What seest thou?

Launce. Him we go to find.
There's not a hair on's head but 'tis a valentine.
Proteus [*bends over him*]. Valentine!
Valentine. No.
Proteus. Who then? his spirit?
Valentine. Neither.
Proteus. What then?
Valentine. Nothing.
Launce. Can nothing speak? Master, shall I strike?
Proteus. Who wouldst thou strike?   200
Launce. Nothing.
Proteus. Villain, forbear.
Launce. Why, sir, I'll strike nothing: I pray you—
[*he lifts his staff*
Proteus. Sirrah, I say, forbear...Friend Valentine,
a word.
Valentine. My ears are stopped, and cannot hear
good news,
So much of bad already hath possessed them.
Proteus. Then in dumb silence will I bury mine,
For they are harsh, untuneable and bad.
Valentine [*looks up*]. Is Silvia dead?
Proteus. No, Valentine.   210
Valentine. No Valentine, indeed, for sacred Silvia.
Hath she forsworn me?
Proteus. No, Valentine.
Valentine. No valentine, if Silvia have forsworn me—
What is your news?
Launce. Sir, there is a proclamation that you are vanished.
Proteus. That thou art banishéd...O, that's the news—
From hence, from Silvia, and from me thy friend.
Valentine. O, I have fed upon this woe already,
And now excess of it will make me surfeit....   220
Doth Silvia know that I am banishéd?

Proteus. Ay, ay: and she hath offered to the doom—
Which, unreversed, stands in effectual force—
A sea of melting pearl, which some call tears;
Those at her father's churlish feet she tendered,
With them, upon her knees, her humble self,
Wringing her hands, whose whiteness so became them,
As if but now they waxéd pale for woe:
But neither bended knees, pure hands held up,
230 Sad sighs, deep groans, nor silver-shedding tears,
Could penetrate her uncompassionate sire;
But Valentine, if he be ta'en, must die....
Besides, her intercession chafed him so,
When she for thy repeal was suppliant,
That to close prison he commanded her,
With many bitter threats of biding there.
  Valentine. No more...unless the next word that
         thou speak'st
Have some malignant power upon my life:
If so...I pray thee breathe it in mine ear,
240 As ending anthem of my endless dolour.
  Proteus. Cease to lament for that thou canst not help,
And study help for that which thou lament'st.
Time is the nurse and breeder of all good;
Here if thou stay, thou canst not see thy love:
Besides, thy staying will abridge thy life:
Hope is a lover's staff—walk hence with that,
And manage it against despairing thoughts:
Thy letters may be here, though thou art hence,
Which, being writ to me, shall be delivered
250 Even in the milk-white bosom of thy love....
                              [*Valentine rises*
The time now serves not to expostulate—
Come, I'll convey thee through the city-gate....
                              [*Proteus leads him away*

And, ere I part with thee, confer at large
Of all that may concern thy love-affairs:
As thou lov'st Silvia, though not for thyself,
Regard thy danger, and along with me.

Valentine. I pray thee, Launce, an if thou seest my boy,
Bid him make haste and meet me at the North-gate.

Proteus. Go, sirrah, find him out....Come, Valentine.

Valentine. O my dear Silvia; hapless Valentine. 260

[they go

Launce. I am but a fool, look you, and yet I have the
wit to think my master is a kind of a knave: but that's all
one, if he be but one knave...He lives not now that knows
me to be in love—yet I am in love—but a team of horse
shall not pluck that from me: nor who 'tis I love: and yet
'tis a woman; but what woman, I will not tell myself: and
yet 'tis a milkmaid: yet 'tis not a maid: for she hath had
gossips: yet 'tis a maid, for she is her master's maid, and
serves for wages.... *[searches his pockets]* She hath more
qualities than a water-spaniel—which is much in a bare 270
Christian.... *[pulls out a paper]* Here is the catalogue of
her condition. '*Inprimis*, She can fetch and carry'...
Why, a horse can do no more; nay, a horse cannot fetch,
but only carry; therefore is she better than a jade.
'*Item*, She can milk'—look you, a sweet virtue in a maid
with clean hands.

SPEED comes up

Speed. How now, Signior Launce! what news with your
mastership?

Launce. With my master's ship? why, it is at sea.

Speed. Well, your old vice still: mistake the word...What 280
news, then, in your paper?

Launce. The black'st news that ever thou heard'st.

Speed. Why, man, how black?

Launce. Why, as black as ink.

Speed. Let me read them.

Launce. Fie on thee jolthead, thou canst not read.

Speed. Thou liest...I can.

Launce. I will try thee: tell me this: who begot thee?

Speed. Marry, the son of my grandfather.

290 *Launce.* O illiterate loiterer; it was the son of thy grand-mother...This proves that thou canst not read.

Speed. Come, fool, come: try me in thy paper.

Launce. There...[*giving the paper*] and Saint Nicholas be thy speed!

Speed. 'Inprimis, She can milk.'

Launce. Ay, that she can.

Speed. 'Item, She brews good ale.'

Launce. And thereof comes the proverb: 'Blessing of your heart, you brew good ale.'

300 *Speed.* 'Item, She can sew.'

Launce. That's as much as to say, 'Can she so?'

Speed. 'Item, She can knit.'

Launce. What need a man care for a stock with a wench, when she can knit him a stock.

Speed. 'Item, She can wash and scour.'

Launce. A special virtue: for then she need not be washed and scoured.

Speed. 'Item, She can spin.'

Launce. Then may I set the world on wheels, when she 310 can spin for her living.

Speed. 'Item, She hath many nameless virtues.'

Launce. That's as much as to say, bastard virtues: that, indeed, know not their fathers; and therefore have no names.

Speed. 'Here follow her vices.'

Launce. Close at the heels of her virtues.

Speed. 'Item, She is not to be — fasting, in respect of her breath.'

Launce. Well...that fault may be mended with a breakfast...Read on.   320

Speed. '*Item*, She hath a sweet mouth.'

Launce. That makes amends for her sour breath.

Speed. '*Item*, She doth talk in her sleep.'

Launce. It's no matter for that; so she †slip not in her
talk.

Speed. '*Item*, She is slow in words.'

Launce. O villain, that set this down among her vices!
To be slow in words is a woman's only virtue: I pray thee,
out with't, and place it for her chief virtue.

Speed. '*Item*, She is proud.'   330

Launce. Out with that too...It was Eve's legacy, and
annot be ta'en from her.

Speed. '*Item*, She hath no teeth.'

Launce. I care not for that neither...because I love crusts

Speed. '*Item*, She is curst.'

Launce. Well...the best is, she hath no teeth to bite.

Speed. '*Item*, She will often praise her liquor.'

Launce. If her liquor be good, she shall: if she will not,
 will; for good things should be praised.

Speed. '*Item*, She is too liberal.'   340

Launce. Of her tongue she cannot; for that's writ down
she is slow of: of her purse she shall not, for that I'll keep
shut: now, of another thing she may, and that cannot I
help....Well, proceed.

Speed. '*Item*, She hath more hair than wit, and more
faults than hairs, and more wealth than faults.'

Launce. Stop there...I'll have her...she was mine, and
not mine, twice or thrice in that last article: rehearse
that once more.

Speed. '*Item*, She hath more hair than wit'—   350

Launce. More hair than wit: it may be I'll prove it...The
cover of the salt hides the salt, and therefore it is more

than the salt; the hair that covers the wit is more than
the wit; for the greater hides the less...What's next?

Speed.—'And more faults than hairs'—

Launce. That's monstrous: O, that that were out!

Speed.—'And more wealth than faults.'

Launce. Why, that word makes the faults gracious...Well,
I'll have her: and if it be a match, as nothing is impossible—

360 *Speed.* What then?

Launce. Why, then will I tell thee—that thy master
stays for thee at the North-gate.

Speed. For me!

Launce. For thee? ay, who art thou? he hath stayed for
a better man than thee.

Speed. And must I go to him?

Launce. Thou must run to him; for thou hast stayed so
long, that going will scarce serve the turn.

Speed. Why didst not tell me sooner? 'pox of your love-

370 letters!   [*he runs off*

Launce. Now will he be swinged for reading my letter...
An unmannerly slave, that will thrust himself into secrets...
I'll after, to rejoice in the boy's correction.   [*he follows*

[3.2.]   *Milan: a room in the Duke's palace*

The DUKE: *THURIO*

Duke. Sir Thurio, fear not but that she will love you,
Now Valentine is banished from her sight.

Thurio. Since his exíle she hath despised me most,
Forsworn my company and railed at me,
That I am desperate of obtaining her.

Duke. This weak impress of love is as a figure
Trenchéd in ice, which with an hour's heat
Dissolves to water and doth lose his form....

A little time will melt her frozen thoughts,
And worthless Valentine shall be forgot.... 10

PROTEUS enters

How now, Sir Proteus! Is your countryman,
According to our proclamation, gone?
Proteus. Gone, my good lord.
Duke. My daughter takes his going grievously!
Proteus. A little time, my lord, will kill that grief.
Duke. So I believe: but Thurio thinks not so...
Proteus, the good conceit I hold of thee—
For thou hast shown some sign of good desert—
Makes me the better to confer with thee.
  Proteus [bows]. Longer than I prove loyal to your
     grace 20
Let me not live to look upon your grace.
Duke. Thou know'st how willingly I would effect
The match between Sir Thurio and my daughter?
Proteus. I do, my lord.
Duke. And also, I think, thou art not ignorant
How she opposes her against my will?
  Proteus. She did, my lord, when Valentine
     was here.
Duke. Ay, and perversely she persévers so...
What might we do to make the girl forget
The love of Valentine, and love Sir Thurio? 30
  Proteus. The best way is to slander Valentine
With falsehood, cowardice, and poor descent:
Three things that women highly hold in hate.
Duke. Ay, but she'll think that it is spoke in hate.
Proteus. Ay, if his enemy deliver it....
Therefore it must with circumstance be spoken
By one whom she esteemeth as his friend.
Duke. Then you must undertake to slander him.

Proteus. And that, my lord, I shall be loath to do...
40 'Tis an ill office for a gentleman,
Especially against his very friend.
   Duke. Where your good word cannot advantage him,
Your slander never can endamage him;
Therefore the office is indifferent,
Being entreated to it by your friend.
   Proteus. You have prevailed, my lord. If I can do it,
By aught that I can speak in his dispraise,
She shall not long continue love to him:
†But say this weed her love from Valentine,
50 It follows not that she will love Sir Thurio.
   Thurio. Therefore, as you unwind her love from him—
Lest it should ravel and be good to none—
You must provide to bottom it on me:
Which must be done, by praising me as much
As you in worth dispraise Sir Valentine.
   Duke. And, Proteus, we dare trust you in this kind
Because we know, on Valentine's report,
You are already Love's firm votary,
And cannot soon revolt and change your mind....
60 Upon this warrant, shall you have access
Where you with Silvia may confer at large....
For she is lumpish, heavy, melancholy,
And—for your friend's sake—will be glad of you;
Where you may temper her, by your persuasion,
To hate young Valentine and love my friend.
   Proteus. As much as I can do, I will effect...
But you, Sir Thurio, are not sharp enough:
You must lay lime to tangle her desires
By wailful sonnets, whose composéd rhymes
70 Should be full-fraught with serviceable vows.
   Duke. Ay,
Much is the force of heaven-bred poesy.

Proteus. Say that upon the altar of her beauty
You sacrifice your tears, your sighs, your heart:
Write till your ink be dry: and with your tears
Moist it again: and frame·some feeling line
That may discover such integrity...
For Orpheus' lute was strung with poets' sinews—
Whose golden touch could soften steel and stones;
Make tigers tame and huge leviathans   80
Forsake unsounded deeps to dance on sands....
After your dire-lamenting elegies,
Visit by night your lady's chamber-window
With some sweet consort; to their instruments
Tune a deploring dump: the night's dead silence
Will well become such sweet-complaining grievance...
This, or else nothing, will inherit her.
  Duke. This discipline shows thou hast been in love.
  Thurio. And thy advice, this night, I'll put in practice:
Therefore, sweet Proteus, my direction-giver,   90
Let us into the city presently
To sort some gentlemen well skilled in music....
I have a sonnet that will serve the turn
To give the onset to thy good advice.
  Duke. About it, gentlemen.   *[he turns to go*
  Proteus [*following*]. We'll wait upon your grace till
       after supper,
And afterward determine our proceedings.
  Duke. Even now about it. I will pardon you.
                    [*The Duke goes in to supper; Proteus and*
                          Thurio leave the palace

[4.1.]   *A highway running through a forest*

Three outlaws, bearing bows and arrows, keep watch from a thicket: VALENTINE and SPEED are seen approaching

1 *Outlaw.* Fellows, stand fast...I see a passenger.
2 *Outlaw.* If there be ten, shrink not, but down with 'em.

  They step forth and cover them with their bows

3 *Outlaw.* Stand, sir, and throw us that you have
  about ye....
If not...we'll make you sit, and rifle you.
Speed. Sir, we are undone; these are the villains
That all the travellers do fear so much.
Valentine [*calm*]. My friends—
1 *Outlaw.* That's not so, sir: we are your enemies.
2 *Outlaw.* Peace...we'll hear him.
10 3 *Outlaw.* Ay, by my beard, will we: for he's a proper man.
Valentine. Then know, that I have little wealth to lose;
A man I am crossed with adversity:
My riches are these poor habiliments,
Of which if you should here disfurnish me,
You take the sum and substance that I have.
2 *Outlaw.* Whither travel you?
Valentine. To Verona.
1 *Outlaw.* Whence came you?
Valentine. From Milan.
20 3 *Outlaw.* Have you long sojourned there?
Valentine. Some sixteen months, and longer might
  have stayed,
If crooked fortune had not thwarted me.
1 *Outlaw.* What, were you banished thence?
Valentine. I was.
2 *Outlaw.* For what offence?

Valentine. For that which now torments me to rehearse;
I killed a man, whose death I much repent.
But yet I slew him manfully in fight,
Without false vantage, or base treachery.

  1 *Outlaw*. Why, ne'er repent it, if it were done so;   30
But were you banished for so small a fault?

  Valentine. I was, and held me glad of such a doom.

  2 *Outlaw*. Have you the tongues?

  Valentine. My youthful travel therein made me happy;
Or else I often had been miserable.

  3 *Outlaw*. By the bare scalp of Robin Hood's fat friar,
This fellow were a king for our wild faction.

  1 *Outlaw*. We'll have him...Sirs, a word. [*they talk apart*

  Speed.   Master, be one of them:
It's an honourable kind of thievery.   40

  Valentine. Peace, villain.

  2 *Outlaw*. Tell us this: have you any thing to take to?

  Valentine. Nothing but my fortune.

  3 *Outlaw*. Know then, that some of us are gentlemen,
Such as the fury of ungoverned youth
Thrust from the company of awful men....
Myself was from Verona banished,
For practising to steal away a lady,
†An heir, and near allied unto the duke.

  2 *Outlaw*. And I from Mantua, for a gentleman   50
Whom, in my mood, I stabbed unto the heart.

  1 *Outlaw*. And I, for such like petty crimes as these....
But to the purpose: for we cite our faults,
That they may hold excused our lawless lives;
And partly, seeing you are beautified
With goodly shape, and by your own report
A linguist, and a man of such perfection
As we do in our quality much want—

  2 *Outlaw*. Indeed, because you are a banished man,

60 Therefore, above the rest, we parley to you:
Are you content to be our general?
To make a virtue of necessity,
And live as we do in this wilderness?

   3 *Outlaw.* What sayst thou? wilt thou be of our consórt?
Say 'ay,' and be the captain of us all:
We'll do thee homage and be ruled by thee,
Love thee as our commander and our king.

    1 *Outlaw.* But if thou scorn our courtesy, thou diest.

    2 *Outlaw.* Thou shalt not live to brag what we have
      offered.

70 *Valentine.* I take your offer, and will live with you,
Provided that you do no outrages
On silly women or poor passengers.

   3 *Outlaw.* No, we detest such vile base practices....
Come, go with us, we'll bring thee to our crew,
And show thee all the treasure we have got;
Which, with ourselves, all rest at thy dispose.

                  [they turn into the forest

[4.2.]   *A wall, with a postern, behind the Duke's palace:*
inside a strip of garden dividing the wall from a lofty
turret; outside, a narrow lane with bushes: a moonlit night

    P*ROTEUS opens the postern and enters the garden*

   Proteus. Already have I been false to Valentine,
And now I must be as unjust to Thurio.
Under the colour of commending him,
I have access my own love to prefer....
But Silvia is too fair, too true, too holy,
To be corrupted with my worthless gifts;
When I protest true loyalty to her,
She twits me with my falsehood to my friend;
When to her beauty I commend my vows,

She bids me think how I have been forsworn   10
In breaking faith with Julia whom I loved;
And notwithstanding all her sudden quips,
The least whereof would quell a lover's hope...
Yet, spaniel-like, the more she spurns my love,
The more it grows, and fawneth on her still;

THURIO and the musicians come up the lane

But here comes Thurio; now must we to her window,
And give some evening music to her ear.
   Thurio [*enters the garden*]. How now, Sir Proteus, are
     you crept before us?
Proteus. Ay, gentle Thurio, for you know that love
Will creep in service where it cannot go.   20
   Thurio. Ay, but I hope, sir, that you love not here.
   Proteus. Sir, but I do: or else I would be hence.
   Thurio. Who? Silvia?
   Proteus.   Ay, Silvia—for your sake.
   Thurio. I thank you for your own...Now, gentlemen,
Let's tune, and to it lustily awhile.

The musicians stand beneath a balcony of the turret: an old
   Host and JULIA, *disguised as a boy, appear in the lane*

   Host. Now, my young guest; methinks you're allicholy;
I pray you, why is it?
   Julia. Marry, mine host, because I cannot be merry.
   Host. Come, we'll have you merry: I'll bring you where
you shall hear music, and see the gentleman that you   30
asked for.   [*they approach the postern*
   Julia. But shall I hear him speak?
   Host. Ay, that you shall.
   Julia. That will be music.   [*the musicians strike up*
   Host. Hark! hark!
   Julia. Is he among these?

Host. Ay: but peace, let's hear 'em.

Song.

Who is Silvia? what is she,
That all our swains commend her?
40   Holy, fair, and wise is she.
The heaven such grace did lend her,
    That she might admiréd be.

Is she kind as she is fair?
For beauty lives with kindness:
Love doth to her eyes repair,
To help him of his blindness:
    And, being helped, inhabits there.

Then to Silvia let us sing,
That Silvia is excelling;
50   She excels each mortal thing,
Upon the dull earth dwelling.
    To her let us garlands bring.

Host. How now! are you sadder than you were before?
How do you, man? the music likes you not.

Julia. You mistake: the musician likes me not.

Host. Why, my pretty youth?

Julia. He plays false, father.

Host. How? out of tune on the strings?

Julia. Not so: but yet so false, that he grieves my very
60 heart-strings.

Host. You have a quick ear.

Julia. Ay, I would I were deaf...it makes me have a
slow heart.

Host. I perceive you delight not in music.

Julia. Not a whit, when it jars so. [*the music begins afresh*

Host. Hark, what fine change is in the music!

Julia. Ay: that change is the spite.

Host. You would have them always play but one thing.

Julia. I would always have one play but one thing....
But, host, doth this Sir Proteus that we talk on   70
Often resort unto this gentlewoman?

Host. I tell you what Launce, his man, told me—he
loved her out of all nick.

Julia. Where is Launce?

Host. Gone to seek his dog, which to-morrow, by his
master's command, he must carry for a present to his lady.

Julia. Peace, stand aside, the company parts.
                              [*they crouch behind a bush*

Proteus [*at the postern*]. Sir Thurio, fear not you. I will
    so plead,
That you shall say my cunning drift excels.

   Thurio. Where meet we?

   Proteus.   At Saint Gregory's well.

   Thurio.   Farewell. 80
         [*Thurio and the musicians go off down the lane*

*A window opens in the turret; SILVIA appears on
                    the balcony*

Proteus. Madam: good even to your ladyship.

Silvia. I thank you for your music, gentlemen.
Who is that that spake?

Proteus. One, lady, if you knew his pure heart's truth,
You would quickly learn to know him by his voice.

Silvia. Sir Proteus, as I take it.

Proteus. Sir Proteus, gentle lady, and your servant.

Silvia. What is your will?

Proteus.   That I may compass yours.

Silvia. You have your wish: my will is even this—
That presently you hie you home to bed...   90
Thou subtle, perjured, false, disloyal man!
Think'st thou I am so shallow, so conceitless,
To be seducéd by thy flattery,

T.G.V. – 5

That hast deceived so many with thy vows?
Return, return, and make thy love amends:
For me—by this pale queen of night I swear!
I am so far from granting thy request,
That I despise thee for thy wrongful suit;
And by and by intend to chide myself
100 Even for this time I spend in talking to thee.
   Proteus. I grant, sweet love, that I did love a lady—
But she is dead:
   (*Julia.*   'Twere false, if I should speak it;
For I am sure she is not buriéd.
   Silvia. Say that she be: yet Valentine thy friend
Survives; to whom—thyself art witness—
I am betrothed; and art thou not ashamed
To wrong him with thy importúnacy?
   Proteus. I likewise hear that Valentine is dead.
   Silvia. And so suppose am I; for in his grave
110 Assure thyself my love is buriéd.
   Proteus. Sweet lady, let me rake it from the earth.
   Silvia. Go to thy lady's grave and call her's thence
Or, at the least, in her's sepúlchre thine.
   (*Julia.* He heard not that.
   Proteus. Madam…if your heart be so obdurate…
Vouchsafe me yet your picture for my love,
The picture that is hanging in your chamber:
To that I'll speak, to that I'll sigh and weep:
For since the substance of your perfect self
120 Is else devoted, I am but a shadow;
And to your shadow—will I make true love.
   (*Julia.* If 'twere a substance, you would, sure, deceive it,
And make it but a shadow, as I am.
   Silvia. I am very loath to be your idol, sir;
But, since your falsehood shall become you well
To worship shadows and adore false shapes,

Send to me in the morning, and I'll send it:
And so, good rest.   [*she shuts her window*

  Proteus.   As wretches have o'ernight
That wait for execution in the morn.

       [*he closes the postern and passes down the lane*

Julia. Host, will you go?   130
  Host. By my halidom, I was fast asleep.
  Julia. Pray you, where lies Sir Proteus?
  Host. Marry, at my house...Trust me, I think 'tis almost day.
  Julia. Not so: but it hath been the longest night,
That e'er I watched, and the most heaviest.   [*they go*

[4.3.]   *EGLAMOUR comes down the lane and halts*
              by the postern

  Eglamour. This is the hour that Madam Silvia
Entreated me to call and know her mind:
There's some great matter she'ld employ me in....
Madam, madam!   [*calling*

    The window opens and SILVIA appears once more

  Silvia.   Who calls?
  Eglamour.   Your servant, and your friend;
One that attends your ladyship's command.
  Silvia. Sir Eglamour, a thousand times good morrow.
  Eglamour. As many, worthy lady, to yourself...
According to your ladyship's impose,
I am thus early come to know what service
It is your pleasure to command me in.   10
  Silvia. O Eglamour, thou art a gentleman—
Think not I flatter, for I swear I do not—
Valiant, wise, remorseful, well-accomplished.
Thou art not ignorant what dear good will
I bear unto the banished Valentine...
Nor how my father would enforce me marry
Vain Thurio—whom my very soul abhors....

Thyself hast loved, and I have heard thee say
No grief did ever come so near thy heart,
20 As when thy lady and thy true love died,
Upon whose grave thou vow'dst pure chastity...
Sir Eglamour...I would to Valentine,
To Mantua, where I hear he makes abode;
And, for the ways are dangerous to pass,
I do desire thy worthy company,
Upon whose faith and honour I repose....
Urge not my father's anger, Eglamour,
But think upon my grief—a lady's grief—
And on the justice of my flying hence,
30 To keep me from a most unholy match,
Which heaven and fortune still rewards with plagues....
I do desire thee, even from a heart
As full of sorrows as the sea of sands,
To bear me company, and go with me:
If not, to hide what I have said to thee,
That I may venture to depart alone.
Eglamour. Madam, I pity much your grievances,
Which since I know they virtuously are placed,
I give consent to go along with you,
40 Recking as little what betideth me,
As much I wish all good befortune you....
When will you go?
Silvia.   This evening coming.
Eglamour. Where shall I meet you?
Silvia.   At Friar Patrick's cell,
Where I intend holy confession.
Eglamour. I will not fail your ladyship: good morrow,
gentle lady.   [_he returns up the lane_
Silvia. Good morrow, kind Sir Eglamour.
                              [_she closes her window_

                Six or seven hours pass

[4.4.] *LAUNCE, with his dog at his heels, comes forth from the postern, and casts himself under a bush, groaning*

Launce [*to the dog*]. When a man's servant shall play the cur with him—look you—it goes hard: one that I brought up of a puppy: one that I saved from drowning, when three or four of his blind brothers and sisters went to it: I have taught him—even as one would say precisely, 'Thus I would teach a dog.' I was sent to deliver him, as a present to Mistress Silvia from my master; and I came no sooner into the dining-chamber, but he steps me to her trencher, and steals her capon's leg...O, 'tis a foul thing, when a cur cannot keep himself in all companies: 10 I would have—as one should say—one that takes upon him to be a dog indeed, to be, as it were, a dog at all things.... If I had not had more wit than he, to take a fault upon me that he did, I think verily he had been hanged for't: sure as I live, he had suffered for't: you shall judge... He thrusts me himself into the company of three or four gentlemen-like dogs, under the duke's table: he had not been there (bless the mark!) a pissing-while, but all the chamber smelt him...'Out with the dog,' says one—'What cur is that?' says another—'Whip him out,' says the third 20 —'Hang him up,' says the duke....I, having been acquainted with the smell before, knew it was Crab; and goes me to the fellow that whips the dogs: 'Friend,' quoth I, 'you mean to whip the dog?' 'Ay, marry, do I,' quoth he. 'You do him the more wrong,' quoth I, ''twas I did the thing you wot of': he makes me no more ado, but whips me out of the chamber...How many masters would do this for his servant? Nay, I'll be sworn, I have sat in the stocks for puddings he hath stol'n, otherwise he had been executed: I have stood on the pillory for geese 30 he hath killed, otherwise he had suffered for't...Thou think'st not of this now...Nay, I remember the trick you served me, when I took my leave of Madam Silvia: did not I bid thee still mark me, and do as I do? when didst thou see me heave up my leg, and make water against a gentlewoman's farthingale? didst thou ever see me do such a trick?

PROTEUS and JULIA (disguised as a boy) pass by

Proteus. Sebastian is thy name: I like thee well, And will employ thee in some service presently.
40 *Julia.* In what you please. I will do what I can.
Proteus. I hope thou wilt...[*he spies Launce*] How now, you whoreson peasant!
Where have you been these two days loitering?
Launce. Marry, sir, I carried Mistress Silvia the dog you bade me.
Proteus. And what says she to my little Jewel?
Launce. Marry, she says your dog was a cur, and tells you currish thanks is good enough for such a present.
Proteus. But she received my dog?
Launce. No, indeed, did she not: here have I brought
50 him back again.
Proteus. What! didst thou offer her this from me?
Launce. Ay sir, the other squirrel was stol'n from me by the hangman boys in the market-place, and then I offered her mine own, who is a dog as big as ten of yours, and therefore the gift the greater.
Proteus. Go, get thee hence, and find my dog again, Or ne'er return again into my sight....
Away, I say...stayest thou to vex me here?
A slave, that still an-end turns me to shame...

[*Launce goes, with Crab behind him*
60 Sebastian, I have entertainéd thee,

Partly that I have need of such a youth,
That can with some discretion do my business...
For 'tis no trusting to yond foolish lout...
But chiefly for thy face and thy behaviour,
Which, if my augury deceive me not,
Witness good bringing up, fortune, and truth:
Therefore know thou, for this I entertain thee....
Go presently, and take this ring with thee,
Deliver it to Madam Silvia...
She loved me well delivered it to me.   70

  Julia. †It seems you loved not her, nor love her token...
                                     [taking the ring

She is dead, belike?
  Proteus.   Not so...I think she lives.
  Julia. Alas!
  Proteus. Why dost thou cry 'alas'?
  Julia. I cannot choose but pity her.
  Proteus. Wherefore shouldst thou pity her?
  Julia. Because, methinks, that she loved you as well
As you do love your lady Silvia...
She dreams on him that has forgot her love—
You dote on her that cares not for your love....   80
'Tis pity love should be so contrary:
And thinking on it makes me cry, 'alas!'
  Proteus. Well...give her that ring, and therewithal
This letter...*[points]* That's her chamber...Tell my lady
I claim the promise for her heavenly picture:
Your message done, hie home unto my chamber,
Where thou shalt find me sad—and solitary.   *[he goes*
  Julia. How many women would do such a message?
Alas, poor Proteus, thou hast entertained
A fox to be the shepherd of thy lambs;   90
Alas, poor fool, why do I pity him
That with his very heart despiseth me?

Because he loves her, he despiseth me—
Because I love him, I must pity him....
This ring I gave him, when he parted from me,
To bind him to remember my good will:
And now am I—unhappy messenger!—
To plead for that, which I would not obtain;
To carry that, which I would have refused;
100 To praise his faith, which I would have dispraised....
I am my master's true confirméd love,
But cannot be true servant to my master,
Unless I prove false traitor to myself....
Yet will I woo for him, but yet so coldly,
As, heaven it knows, I would not have him speed....

SILVIA comes from the postern

Gentlewoman, good day: I pray you be my mean
To bring me where to speak with Madam Silvia.
  Silvia. What would you with her, if that I be she?
  Julia. If you be she, I do entreat your patience
110 To hear me speak the message I am sent on.
  Silvia. From whom?
  Julia. From my master, Sir Proteus, madam.
  Silvia. O...he sends you for a picture?
  Julia. Ay, madam.
  Silvia [*calling*]. Ursula, bring my picture there.
                        [*the maid brings the picture*
Go give your master this: tell him from me,
One Julia, that his changing thoughts forget,
Would better fit his chamber than this shadow.
  Julia. Madam, please you peruse this letter...
120 Pardon me, madam, I have unadvised
Delivered you a paper that I should not...
              [*she takes it back in haste and gives another*
This is the letter to your ladyship.

Silvia. I pray thee, let me look on that again.

Julia. It may not be: good madam, pardon me.

Silvia. There, hold...

[*she tears the letter across and returns it*

I will not look upon your master's lines:

I know they are stuffed with protestations,

And full of new-found oaths, which he will break

As easily as I do tear his paper.

Julia. Madam, he sends your ladyship this ring.   130

Silvia. The more shame for him, that he sends it me;

For I have heard him say a thousand times

His Julia gave it him at his departure:

Though his false finger have profaned the ring,

Mine shall not do his Julia so much wrong.

Julia. She thanks you.

Silvia. What sayst thou?

Julia. I thank you, madam, that you tender her:

Poor gentlewoman, my master wrongs her much.

Silvia. Dost thou know her?   140

Julia. Almost as well as I do know myself....

To think upon her woes, I do protest

That I have wept a hundred several times.

Silvia. Belike she thinks that Proteus hath forsook her?

Julia. I think she doth: and that's her cause of sorrow

Silvia. Is she not passing fair?

Julia. She hath been fairer, madam, than she is;

When she did think my master loved her well,

She, in my judgement, was as fair as you....

But since she did neglect her looking-glass,   150

And threw her sun-expelling mask away,

The air hath starved the roses in her cheeks,

And pinched the lily-tincture of her face,

That now she is become as black as I.

Silvia. How tall was she?

Julia. About my stature: for, at Pentecost,
When all our pageants of delight were played,
Our youth got me to play the woman's part,
And I was trimmed in Madam Julia's gown,
160 Which servéd me as fit, by all men's judgement,
As if the garment had been made for me:
Therefore, I know she is about my height.
And at that time I made her weep agood,
For I did play a lamentable part....
Madam, 'twas Ariadne, passioning
For Theseus' perjury and unjust flight;
Which I so lively acted with my tears...
That my poor mistress, movéd therewithal,
Wept bitterly...and, would I might be dead,
170 If I in thought felt not her very sorrow.
   Silvia. She is beholding to thee, gentle youth.
Alas, poor lady! desolate and left;
I weep myself to think upon thy words...
Here, youth: there is my purse; I give thee this
For thy sweet mistress' sake, because thou lov'st her.
Farewell.
   Julia. And she shall thank you for't, if e'er you
        know her....   [*Silvia goes*
A virtuous gentlewoman, mild, and beautiful....
I hope my master's suit will be but cold,
180 Since she respects my mistress' love so much....
Alas, how love can trifle with itself:
Here is her pìcture...[*she sits*] Let me see. I think
If I had such a tire, this face of mine
Were full as lovely as is this of hers;
And yet the painter flattered her a little,
Unless I flatter with myself too much....
Her hair is auburn, mine is perfect yellow;
If that be all the difference in his love,

I'll get me such a coloured periwig:
Her eyes are grey as glass, and so are mine: 190
Ay, but her forehead's low, and mine's as high:
What should it be that he respects in her,
But I can make respective in myself,
If this fond Love were not a blinded god?   *[she rises*
Come, shadow, come, and take this shadow up,
For 'tis thy rival: O thou senseless form,
Thou shalt be worshipped, kissed, loved, and adored;
And, were there sense in his idolatry,
My substance should be statue in thy stead....
I'll use thee kindly, for thy mistress' sake   200
That used me so...or else, by Jove I vow,
I should have scratched out your unseeing eyes,
To make my master out of love with thee.

                                   [she bears away the picture

[5.1.]   *An abbey near Milan: evening*

     EGLAMOUR, *cloaked and spurred, awaits Silvia*

Eglamour. The sun begins to gild the western sky,
And now it is about the very hour
That Silvia, at Friar Patrick's cell, should meet me.
She will not fail; for lovers break not hours,
Unless it be to come before their time—
So much they spur their expedition....

          SILVIA approaches in haste

See, where she comes...Lady, a happy evening!
     Silvia. Amen, amen...go on, good Eglamour,
Out at the postern by the abbey-wall;
I fear I am attended by some spies.   10
     Eglamour. Fear not: the forest is not three leagues off.
If we recover that, we are sure enough. *[they quit the abbey*

[5.2.]   *Milan: a room in the Duke's palace*

THURIO: PROTEUS, *with* JULIA (*as* SEBASTIAN)
in attendance

Thurio. Sir Proteus, what says Silvia to my suit?
Proteus. O sir, I find her milder than she was,
And yet she takes exceptions at your person.
Thurio. What?—that my leg is too long?
Proteus. No, that it is too little.
Thurio. I'll wear a boot, to make it somewhat rounder.
(*Julia.* But love will not be spurred to what it loathes.
Thurio. What says she to my face?
Proteus. She says it is a fair one.
10   *Thurio.* Nay then the wanton lies: my face is black.
Proteus. But pearls are fair; and the old saying is,
Black men are pearls in beauteous ladies' eyes.
(*Julia.* 'Tis true, such pearls as put out ladies' eyes,
For I had rather wink than look on them.
Thurio. How likes she my discourse?
Proteus. Ill, when you talk of war.
Thurio. But well, when I discourse of love and peace.
(*Julia.* But better, indeed, when you hold your peace.
Thurio. What says she to my valour?
20   *Proteus.* O sir, she makes no doubt of that.
(*Julia.* She needs not, when she knows it cowardice.
Thurio. What says she to my birth?
Proteus. That you are well derived.
(*Julia.* True: from a gentleman to a fool.
Thurio. Considers she my possessions?
Proteus. O, ay: and pities them.
Thurio. Wherefore?
(*Julia.* That such an ass should owe them.
Proteus. That they are out by lease.
30   *Julia.* Here comes the duke.

The DUKE enters, in haste

Duke. How now, Sir Proteus! how now, Thurio!
Which of you saw Sir Eglamour of late?
  Thurio. Not I.
  Proteus.   Nor I.
  Duke.   Saw you my daughter?
  Proteus.   Neither.
  Duke. Why then,
She's fled unto that peasant Valentine;
And Eglamour is in her company:
'Tis true...for Friar Laurence met them both,
As he in penance wandered through the forest:
Him he knew well: and guessed that it was she,
But, being masked, he was not sure of it....   40
Besides, she did intend confession
At Patrick's cell this even—and there she was not....
These likelihoods confirm her flight from hence;
Therefore, I pray you, stand not to discourse,
But mount you presently, and meet with me
Upon the rising of the mountain-foot
That leads towards Mantua, whither they are fled:
Dispatch—sweet gentlemen!—and follow me.
                                        [*he hurries out*
  Thurio. Why, this it is to be a peevish girl,
That flies her fortune when it follows her: 50
I'll after; more to be revenged on Eglamour
Than for the love of reckless Silvia. [*he follows the Duke*
  Proteus. And I will follow, more for Silvia's love
Than hate of Eglamour that goes with her.
                                        [*he follows Thurio*
  Julia. And I will follow, more to cross that love
Than hate for Silvia that is gone for love.
                                        [*she follows Proteus*

[5.3.]   *The highway in the forest*

SILVIA, *in the hands of the Outlaws*

1 *Outlaw.* Come, come, be patient: we must bring you
    to our captain.
Silvia. A thousand more mischances than this one
Have learned me how to brook this patiently.
2 *Outlaw.* Come, bring her away.
1 *Outlaw.* Where is the gentleman that was with her?
3 *Outlaw.* Being nimble-footed, he hath outrun us....
But Moses and Valerius follow him:
Go thou with her to the west end of the wood,
There is our captain: we'll follow him that's fled—
10 The thicket is beset, he cannot 'scape.
1 *Outlaw.* Come, I must bring you to our
    captain's cave....
Fear not: he bears an honourable mind,
And will not use a woman lawlessly.
Silvia. O Valentine...this I endure for thee.

[5.4.]   *They pass into the wood:* VALENTINE
            comes slowly along the highway

Valentine. How use doth breed a habit in a man!
This shadowy desert, unfrequented woods,
I better brook than flourishing peopled towns:
Here can I sit alone, unseen of any,
And to the nightingale's complaining notes
Tune my distresses and record my woes....
O thou that dost inhabit in my breast,
Leave not the mansion so long tenantless,
Lest, growing ruinous, the building fall,
10 And leave no memory of what it was.
Repair me with thy presence, Silvia:
Thou gentle nymph, cherish thy forlorn swain....

He muses: cries and the sound of blows are heard

What halloing and what stir is this to-day?
These are my mates, that make their wills their law,
Have some unhappy passenger in chase;
They love me well: yet I have much to do,
To keep them from uncivil outrages....
Withdraw thee, Valentine; who's this comes here?

*He withdraws: SILVIA, in disarray, comes from the wood,
    PROTEUS and JULIA (as SEBASTIAN) following*

Proteus. Madam, this service I have done for you—
Though you respect not aught your servant doth—   20
To hazard life and rescue you from him
That would have forced your honour and your love.
Vouchsafe me, for my meed, but one fair look:
A smaller boon than this I cannot beg,
And less than this, I am sure, you cannot give.
  (Valentine. How like a dream is this! I see—and hear...
Love, lend me patience to forbear awhile.
  Silvia. O miserable, unhappy that I am!
  Proteus. Unhappy were you, madam, ere I came:
But, by my coming, I have made you happy.   30
  Silvia. By thy approach thou mak'st me most
      unhappy.
  (Julia. And me, when he approacheth to your
      presence.
  Silvia. Had I been seizéd by a hungry lion,
I would have been a breakfast to the beast,
Rather than have false Proteus rescue me:
O, heaven be judge, how I love Valentine,
Whose life's as tender to me as my soul—
And full as much (for more there cannot be!)
I do detest false perjured Proteus...
Therefore be gone, solicit me no more.   40

Proteus. What dangerous action, stood it next to death,
Would I not undergo for one calm look?
O, 'tis the curse in love, and still approved,
When women cannot love where they're beloved.
   Silvia. When Proteus cannot love where he's beloved...
Read over Julia's heart—thy first best love—
†For whose dear sake thou didst then rend thy faith
Into a thousand oaths; and, all those oaths
Descended into perjury—to love me.
50 Thou hast no faith left now, unless thou'dst two,
And that's far worse than none: better have none
Than plural faith, which is too much by one...
Thou counterfeit, to thy true friend!
   Proteus.   In love,
Who respects friend?
   Silvia.   All men but Proteus.
   Proteus. Nay, if the gentle spirit of moving words
Can no way change you to a milder form...
I'll woo you like a soldier, at arms' end,
And love you 'gainst the nature of love...force ye.
   Silvia. O heaven!
   Proteus [*seizing her*].   I'll force thee yield to
   my desire.
60 *Valentine.* Ruffian! [*leaping out upon him*] let go that
   rude uncivil touch,
Thou friend of an ill fashion!
   Proteus [*falling back*].   Valentine!
   Valentine. Thou common friend, that's without faith
   or love—
For such is a friend now: treacherous man,
Thou hast beguiled my hopes; nought but mine eye
Could have persuaded me: now I dare not say
I have one friend alive; thou wouldst disprove me...
†Who should be trusted, when one's own right hand

Is perjured to the bosom? Proteus,
I am sorry I must never trust thee more,
But count the world a stranger for thy sake: 70
The private wound is deepest: O time, most accurst...
'Mongst all foes that a friend should be the worst!
  Proteus. My shame and guilt confounds me...
Forgive me, Valentine...if hearty sorrow
Be a sufficient ransom for offence,
I tender't here; I do as truly suffer,
As e'er I did commit.
  Valentine.   Then I am paid:
And once again I do receive thee honest;
Who by repentance is not satisfied,
Is nor of heaven nor earth; for these are pleased: 80
By penitence th'Eternal's wrath's appeased...
And that my love may appear plain and free,
All that was mine in Silvia I give thee.
  Julia. O me, unhappy!   [*she swoons*
  Proteus. Look to the boy.
  Valentine. Why, boy!
Why wag! how now? what's the matter? Look up: speak.
  Julia. O good sir, my master charged me to deliver a
ring to Madam Silvia...which, out of my neglect, was
never done.   90
  Proteus. Where is that ring, boy?
  Julia. Here 'tis....this is it.
  Proteus. How! let me see....   [*taking it*
Why this is the ring I gave to Julia.
  Julia. O, cry you mercy, sir, I have mistook:
This is the ring you sent to Silvia. [*she proffers another ring*
  Proteus. But how cam'st thou by this ring? at my depart
I gave this unto Julia.
  Julia. And Julia herself did give it me—
And Julia herself hath brought it hither.   100

Proteus. How! Julia!

Julia. Behold her that gave aim to all thy oaths,
And entertained 'em deeply in her heart....
How oft hast thou with perjury cleft the root!
O Proteus, let this habit make thee blush....
Be thou ashamed that I have took upon me
Such an immodest raiment; if shame live
In a disguise of love!
It is the lesser blot, modesty finds,
110 Women to change their shapes than men their minds.

Proteus. Than men their minds? 'tis true...O heaven,
    were man
But constant, he were perfect; that one error
Fills him with faults...makes him run through all th'sins;
Inconstancy falls off ere it begins:
What is in Silvia's face, but I may spy
More fresh in Julia's with a constant eye?

Valentine. Come, come: a hand from either:

                    [*he joins their hands*
Let me be blest to make this happy close:
'Twere pity two such friends should be long foes.
120 *Proteus.* Bear witness, heaven, I have my wish for ever.

Julia. And I mine.

Outlaws appear, haling along the DUKE *and* THURIO

Outlaw. A prize...a prize...a prize!

Valentine. Forbear, forbear, I say: it is my lord the duke....
Your grace is welcome to a man disgraced,
Banishéd Valentine.

Duke.   Sir Valentine!

Thurio. Yonder is Silvia: and Silvia's mine.

                    [*he makes towards her*
Valentine. Thurio give back; or else embrace thy death:
Come not within the measure of my wrath:

Do not name Silvia thine: if once again,
Verona shall not hold thee...Here she stands,   130
Take but possession of her—with a touch...
I dare thee but to breathe upon my love!
  Thurio. Sir Valentine, I care not for her, I:
I hold him but a fool that will endanger
His body for a girl that loves him not:
I claim her not, and therefore she is thine.
  Duke. The more degenerate and base art thou,
To make such means for her as thou hast done,
And leave her on such slight conditions....
                              [*he turns from him*
Now, by the honour of my ancestry,   140
I do applaud thy spirit, Valentine,
And think thee worthy of an empress' love:
Know then, I here forget all former griefs,
Cancel all grudge, repeal thee home again,
Plead a new state in thy unrivalled merit,
To which I thus subscribe: Sir Valentine,
Thou art a gentleman, and well derived.
Take thou thy Silvia, for thou hast deserved her.
  Valentine. I thank your grace; the gift hath made
      me happy:
I now beseech you—for your daughter's sake—   150
To grant one boon that I shall ask of you.
  Duke. I grant it—for thine own—whate'er it be.
  Valentine. These banished men, that I have kept withal,
Are men endued with worthy qualities:
Forgive them what they have committed here,
And let them be recalled from their exíle:
They are reforméd, civil, full of good,
And fit for great employment, worthy lord.
  Duke. Thou hast prevailed, I pardon them and thee:
Dispose of them, as thou know'st their deserts....   160

Come, let us go. We will include all jars
With triumphs, mirth, and rare solemnity.
  Valentine. And, as we walk along, I dare be bold
With our discourse to make your grace to smile....
What think you of this page, my lord?
  Duke. I think the boy hath grace in him—he blushes.
  Valentine. I warrant you, my lord, more grace than boy.
  Duke. What mean you by that saying?
  Valentine. Please you, I'll tell you as we pass along,
170 That you will wonder what hath fortunéd:
Come Proteus, 'tis your penance but to hear
The story of your loves discoveréd....
That done, our day of marriage shall be yours—
One feast, one house, one mutual happiness.

They pass out of sight along the highway

THE COPY FOR *THE TWO GENTLEMEN OF VERONA*, 1623

There is no Quarto for *The Two Gentlemen* and the play probably first saw the light of print in the First Folio. The most striking bibliographical features of this text, features which it shares with *The Merry Wives*, its successor in the Folio, are the complete absence of stage-directions and the almost complete absence of entries and exits for characters, except at the beginning or end of the scenes. Despite the claim in the Folio sub-title that the plays of that volume were 'truely set forth, according to their first originall,' it is hardly possible that a text in this condition can have been printed from theatrical prompt-copy, still less from the author's manuscript. No company could have acted the play as it stands. Yet it is not difficult to see how such a text could have been made up for a printer.

For stage-performances in Shakespeare's day three sorts of manuscript material were necessary. First, there was the prompt-copy, which contained at least the bare minimum of stage-directions together with precise indications for the entry of characters and generally, though being less important not so invariably, the indications for exit. Second, there were the players' parts, which were transcribed from the prompt-copy, with the cues, and handed out to the actors for the memorising of their lines. Third, there was the 'plot' or 'plat' of the play, a foolscap sheet (often pasted on to a board so that it could be hung up at a convenient place behind the scenes) on which were written the names of the characters appearing in each scene and of the actors playing them, in the order in which they were to come on. On this sheet the scene-divisions were marked by lines ruled across it, while occasionally act-divisions were also indicated in similar fashion. It is important to remember that these scene-divisions were theatrical and not literary in character, that is to say they occurred when one group of players left the stage to make room for another, even when the action was continuous and the *mise en scène* unaltered. In a word the rules across the 'plot' were *exeunt omnes* lines. We believe that the 'copy' for *The Two Gentlemen* was made up by stringing together players' parts and arranging them in acts and scenes by the aid of a 'plot.'

This hypothesis at any rate explains many peculiarities of the Folio text. It explains, for example, the absence of stage-directions, and the paucity of the exits and entries. The latter feature is particularly instructive. The only exits found are those at the end of the scenes and at four other places where it would be obvious to a compositor or copyist of average intelligence that the context demands one. The entries are even more extraordinary. In fact there are no proper entries at all, merely lists at the head of each scene of the characters to appear in it, in the order of their appearance. Thus 2. 4. is headed 'Enter Valentine, Siluia, Speed, Duke, Protheus,' although the Duke does not enter until l. 46 or Proteus until l. 97. Now these lists of characters, arranged in the order of entry, correspond very closely with the lists found in the extant 'plots' of the period, except of course that the players' names are omitted. If we suppose that the prompt-copy of *The Two Gentlemen* was lost, that Heminge and Condell supplied Jaggard instead with the players' parts and the 'plot,' and that a scribe was employed to make up copy for the compositors from these materials, the result would be just such a text as now stands second in the Folio.

Editors have uniformly remarked upon the comparative straightforwardness of this text, by which presumably they mean that it is freer than most from 'misprints,' incorrect verse-lining and similar phenomena; and they have sometimes argued from this that the printer's copy was probably author's manuscript. We draw the opposite conclusion. In players' parts the irregularities and obscurities of the prompt-copy would be smoothed out, and a text derived therefrom would be virtually a clean copy. Where words were illegible, the players could refer to the author for light or, failing that, substitute makeshifts of their own in order to give sense. Textual difficulties might be safely left alone in the prompt-copy, but in the 'parts' they were bound to be tackled, since intelligibility is the first requisite of stage-performance. Doubtless the comparative simplicity of the language in this early play is one cause of its freedom from verbal cruxes, as Malone pointed out. The main cause, however, we suggest, is that it was printed from a transcript in which most of the puzzles which prompt-copy would have set a compositor had been solved or eliminated. Nevertheless, though a transcript from players' parts might be free from ambiguities, it by no means follows that it would be free from corruption. Actors, for instance, are prone to 'gag,' and we shall draw attention in our notes to certain passages which may have suffered from this cause.

But 'gag' is not the worst. There can be little doubt that the text, as a whole, whether in the original prompt-copy or in the process of making-out the players' parts, has been hacked about and drastically abridged in order to meet the requirements of a particular performance or company. In the nature of the case the bibliographical evidence for this is slight, but the literary evidence is so strong as to be overwhelming. The details will be brought out in the notes. A glance at two passages is enough to establish a *prima facie* case here:—

(i) 2. 4. 194–6, which the F. prints:

It is mine. or *Valentines* praiſe?
Her true perfection, or my falſe tranſgreſſion?
That makes me reaſonleſſe, to reaſon thus?

The first line is hopeless. Most editors read 'Is it' for

'It is' and bolder spirits, like Theobald, rewrite the
line as
                Is it mine eye or Valentino's praise.

But the F. period, 'It is' and the absolutely unmetrical
character of the line as it stands render legitimate
emendation impossible. We are, therefore, forced to
conclude that the text has been tampered with at this
point, in order to shorten the soliloquy. Other instances
of 'cutting' scarcely less glaring are to be found at
3. 2. 75–8 and 4. 1. 55–8.

(ii) 5. 4. 88–90, which the F. prints as prose, thus:

Iul. O good ſir, my maſter charg'd me to deliuer a ring
to Madam Siluia: ẃ (out of my neglect) was neuer done.

The occurrence of an isolated prose speech in the middle
of a verse scene raises suspicions. But suspicion becomes
certainty when it is observed that

          Which, out of my neglect, was never done

is a line of verse. In other words, the adapter has here
tampered with the text, using, however, a scrap of
Shakespeare's original to help patch the rent.

The presence of the adapter's hand serves to explain
most if not all the dramatic anomalies, and they are
many, in this strange text. A brief enquiry into how he
worked will summarise the conclusions scattered throughout the notes. Scenes are curtailed. In 2. 2. and 5. 3.,
for example, we are presented with what are apparently
nothing but the conclusions of longer scenes in the original,
the adapter attempting to conceal his traces by writing
a few lines of prose as an introduction. Whole scenes are
omitted. This explains the confusion of time-sequence,
which is a noticeable feature of the transmitted text. The
'time,' for instance, of 3. 1. is ridiculous as it stands; but
imagine an interval-scene between ll. 187 and 188, and
all would be well. Similarly, an interval-scene is needed
between 4. 3. and 4. 4. A somewhat different example
of the same kind of thing is found in 4. 4. where Julia is

one moment at the foot of Silvia's tower and the next in her chamber (v. note 4. 4. 105). It is to be suspected, moreover, that portions of two or more original scenes have been woven together in the manufacture of the infamous finale (v. head-note 5. 4.). In work like this an adapter will naturally have to write a number of link-passages of his own; sometimes these are in prose, sometimes in verse—or what passes as such. Again, drastic abridgment is bound to affect character. Julia's father (v. note 1. 2. 131) probably appeared in the original, while we can be certain that Sir Eglamour's conduct in the forest was different (v. pp. xvi–xvii), to say nothing of the conduct of Valentine and Proteus in the last scene. Finally the confusion of names, e.g. 'Panthion' for 'Pan-thino,' 'duke' for 'emperor,' 'Padua' for 'Milan,' etc. may be set down to the same cause (v. notes 1. 3. 1, 27; 2. 5. 1).

The normal length of a play for the London stage in Elizabethan days was about 3000 lines; the received text of *The Two Gentlemen* contains some 2380 lines. After what has just been said it should not be difficult to believe that at least 600 lines of the original have disappeared. Did the adapter cut still deeper than this in order to make room for lengthy additions of his own? It is impossible to answer positively; but we have strong suspicions that he did. Adaptation for a particular company might carry with it alterations to fit a new cast. Now there are two clowns in this text, and the difference in their quality is striking, to say the least of it. Launce is humorous, in the true Shakespearian manner, and his sallies, some of which we have been able to restore, bite almost every time. But Speed is a poor stick, without character, and he has not a single witty thing to say from beginning to end. In short, we think that Speed may be the creation or re-creation of the adapter (cf. notes 1. 1. 92; 2. 1. 73–4; 2. 4. 7; 2. 5. 1; 3. 1. 295; 5. 4. 1). If so, he was forgotten in 5. 4., while the 'Padua' scene (2. 5.) may be taken as a specimen of the adapter's unaided work-manship—there is nothing in it, nothing at all.

It was a pleasure to find, after these notes had been made up, that a writer in *The Shakespeare League Journal* (Nov. 1920) had independently, and from the acting point of view, arrived at our main conclusions. 'The piece,' she says, 'appears to have been subjected to the process known as "tightening"; it is a short play and it may well be that, in order to bring it within the limits of some particular bill, it was cut down, some speeches being curtailed and others cut out altogether. This would partly, if not entirely, account for the imperfect psychology of the later scenes which makes acting so difficult, and would go far to explain the baldness of the dialogue in parts.'

[1921]   D. W.

P.S. [1955]. The foregoing note is now quite out of date. The theory of assembled texts, for instance, is now generally discredited. See on this Greg, *The Editorial Problem in Shakespeare*, pp. 134–8.

NOTES

All significant departures from the Folio, including important emendations in punctuation, are recorded; the name of the critic who first suggested a reading being placed in brackets. Illustrative spellings and misprints are quoted from the Good Quarto texts or from the Folio where no Good Quarto exists. The line-numeration for reference to plays not yet issued in this edition is that used in Bartlett's *Concordance*.

F., unless otherwise specified, stands for the First Folio; T.I. and Facs. = the Textual Introduction and the Facsimile of a passage from the 'Shakespearian' Addition to *Sir Thomas More*, both to be found in the *Tempest* volume; N.E.D. = *The New English Dictionary*; Sh. Eng. = *Shakespeare's England*; S.D. = Stage-direction; G. = Glossary; Daniel = *Time-Analysis of the plots of Shakespeare's Plays*, P. A. Daniel, New Shak. Soc.

Characters in the Play. Based upon 'The names of all the Actors,' found at the end of the F. text. Variants: 'Duke of Milan' for 'Duke'; 'Proteus' for 'Protheus'; 'Antonio' for 'Anthonio'; 'Panthino' for 'Panthion' (v. note 1. 3. 1); 'Servants, musicians' added to the list.

Acts and Scenes. F. divides throughout, and is followed by all modern editors. But F. divisions are probably taken from the playhouse 'plot' (v. pp. 77–8 and T.I. §3).

Punctuation. Less delicate than that found in *The Tempest*, as we should expect in an early play; but careful on the whole. It is not surprising to find good punctuation in a text taken, as we believe, from players' parts, since if dramatic pointing were not reproduced in the 'parts' it would be futile. We have occasionally used a semi-colon for a F. colon and *vice versa*.

Stage-directions. None in the F., v. pp. 77–8.

22. *Leander* cf. 3. 1. 120. These references to Mar-
lowe's *Hero and Leander* which was entered in the
Stationers' Register in 1593, after the author's death,
have been taken by some as proof that the play belongs
to a later date. All they indicate, however, is that
Shakespeare may have seen the poem in MS., a likely
thing enough since there is a high probability that the
two dramatists were working together at some period
before 1593. For the question of date v. note 3. 1. 170–
87.

43. *dwells,* F. 'dwels;'

54. *shipped* Both Valentine and Proteus proceed
from Verona to Milan by ship (cf. 2. 2. 14; 2. 4. 185),
which is impossible, but it is noteworthy that Valentine
returns homewards by land, and that Julia clearly intends
a journey on foot (2. 7. 8–10, 35). Geography was not
Shakespeare's strong point, but the confusion may well
have been aggravated by the abridger.

62. *farewell* One of the F.'s four internal 'Exits'
occurs at the end of this line, v. p. 78.

65. *leave* (Pope) F. 'loue'; an *e:o* error,'leue' taken
as 'loue.' v. T.I. p. xlii and cf. note 4. 4. 71.

73. *sheep,* quibble upon 'ship.'

75. *An if* F. 'And if'

76. *I a sheep* (F2) F. 'I Sheepe'

78. *my horns are his horns,* etc. The point of the jest is
obscure—possibly a reference to 'Little Boy Blue.'

91. *baa* quibble upon 'bah!'

92. *gav'st thou my letter to Julia?* It is remarkable that
Proteus should employ Valentine's servant as his go-
between rather than his own man, Launce. Lucetta
confirms this at 1. 2. 38. We hear nothing of Launce
until he appears in 2. 3. and Proteus' words 'I must go
send some better messenger' (1. 1. 147) make it possible
that he first engaged Launce after Speed's departure,

though Speed, in a suspect scene however (v. p. 81), welcomes Launce to 'Padua' (2. 5. 1) as an old friend and Proteus' servant. Pope placed the whole of this dialogue between Proteus and Speed in the margin as 'interpolated by the players,' and it is quite conceivable that we have here an addition by the adapter, v. p. 81 and notes 2.1.73–4; 2.4.7; 2.5.1; 3.1.295; 5.4.1. Lucetta's words, which occur in a verse-scene untouched by the adapter, show, however, that a 'Sir Valentine's page' figured in the original text.

95. *a laced mutton* i.e. a strumpet (N.E.D.). v. G. It is strange that Proteus should tolerate such language from a servant in reference to his lady.

108. *But what said she?* etc. F. '*Pro.* But what ſaid ſhe?/*Sp.* I./*Pro.* Nod-I, why that's noddy.' If the text was made up of players' parts and their cues, the confusion is readily explained. Speed's nod, indicated no doubt in the prompt-copy, would not necessarily be in his part, while the parts alone, without the cues, would give 'Nod-I' twice over. Speed's explanation (l. 111) confirms our reading. Theobald reads '*Pro.* But what said she? did she nod?/*Speed* [*first nodding*] Ay.'

119–20. *nothing...noddy* Note the quibble.

133–37. *Sir, I could...hard as steel.* We have preserved the F. arrangement, as doggerel may be intended; but ll. 139–40 are also printed as verse. It must have been difficult at times for a compositor, or copyist, to distinguish between prose and verse in players' parts, which were written on narrow slips of paper.

134. *ducat* i.e. about 3/6, seven times the 'testern' Proteus had just given him.

141. *testerned* (F2) F. 'cestern'd' (i.e. cisterned!).

I. 2.

9. *Sir Eglamour* It is curious that Silvia also has a friend of this name, and that her praise of him (4. 3. 11–13) has points of likeness with Lucetta's depreciatory

comment. Is it possible that they were the same person in the original?

12. *Mercatio* Perhaps a misprint for 'Mercutio.'

30. *Fire* A dissyllable, as frequently elsewhere in Shakespeare, cf. 2. 7. 22.

33–41. Note the versification here: seven unrhymed three-foot lines, followed by a couplet of rhyming alexandrines. F. prints ll. 38–9 as one, but Shakespeare's intention was probably to adhere to the three-foot pattern.

50. *That...ruminate* F. reads 'Exit' at the end of this line, v. p. 78.

68. *Is it* (Capell) F. 'Is't'

69–70. *meat...maid* a quibble, 'meat' being pronounced as 'mate.' Cf. *M.W.W.* note 5. 5. 115 and Wyld, *Hist. of Mod. Colloquial English*, p. 210.

73–4. three-foot lines.

80–97. *Give me a note* etc. For the understanding of this dialogue and the accompanying stage-business, it is necessary to follow closely the series of quibbles upon which they turn. It will, therefore, be more convenient to explain them here than in the G.:—*note* (i) i.e. of music, (ii) a letter in reply to Proteus; *set* (i) set to music, (ii) write; 84 *burden* (i) load, (ii) refrain; 86 *I cannot reach so high* (i) it is beyond the compass of my voice, (ii) he is of too high a rank for me; 88, 89 *tune* (i) correct pitch, (ii) temper, mood, humour; 91, 93 *sharp, flat* obvious quibbles, denoting a pinch and a slap; 94 *descant* i.e. variations; 95 *mean* (i) tenor (possibly Proteus is meant), (ii) Lucetta's 'moan' (cf. *M.N.D.* 5. 1. 330); 96 *bass*, with a quibble upon 'base,' i.e. low conduct; 97 *bid the base* a phrase from the game of prisoner's base, meaning that one of the players challenges the players on the opposite side to pursue him; thus leaving the prisoner at the base free to escape. Proteus is the 'prisoner'; Lucetta 'bids the base' by challenging Julia to pursue her.

82. *the tune of 'Light o' love'* Cf. *Ado* 3. 4. 38 "Light o' love,' that goes without a burden'

91-3. three-foot lines; cf. ll. 33-41.

96. *your unruly* F. 'you vnruly'

98. *babble* possibly for 'bauble'; both 'babble' and 'bauble' could be spelt 'bable' in the 16th century.

106. *injurious wasps* i.e. her fingers.

121. *fearful-hanging* (Delius) F. 'fearfull, hanging'

130. *Madam* Printed with l. 131 in F. Possibly actor's 'gag,' v. p. 79.

131. *your father* This and 1. 3. 48 are the sole references to Julia's father in the received text. At 2. 7. 86-7 Julia appears to be an orphan. The death of a father would add pathos to her figure; his character and the reference to his decease, which perhaps occurred in 2. 2., have, probably, been 'cut' by the abridger.

137. *month's* a dissyllable; probably spelt 'moneths' in the original. F. gives 'moneths' at 4. 1. 21.

1. 3.

1. *Panthino* F. gives two forms of this name. We get 'Panthion' in 'The names of all the Actors' and in the scene-headings of 2. 2. and 2. 3. 'Panthino' occurs in the scene-heading of 1. 3., probably because it is so spelt in the opening line of the scene. The name appears again in 1. 3. 76, where it is misprinted 'Panthmo' which proves that 'Panthino' was the reading of the 'copy' at that point. In short, the evidence suggests that 'Panthino' was the spelling of Antonio's 'part,' while 'Panthion' was that of the 'plot' material (v. pp. 77-8). We have followed Capell, and printed it 'Panthino' throughout.

2. *my brother* Another mysterious character, who possibly figured in the original.

7. *out:* F. 'out.'

24. *whither* F. 'whether'; a Shakespearian spelling, also found at 3. 1. 51 and frequent elsewhere.

27. *the emperor* The reigning monarch of Milan is

five times called 'emperor' in this scene (cf. ll. 38, 41, 58, 67); Launce refers to 'the Imperial's court' at 2. 3. 4; and he appears to speak of himself as 'emperor' at 2. 4. 75 and of his daughter as 'empress' in the previous line and again at 5.4.142. On the other hand, he is styled 'Duke' in 'The names of all the Actors,' in all scene-headings and prefixes, but only three times in the text itself, viz. twice in Launce's prose speech (4. 4. 17, 21) and once in a line of 'verse' (5. 4. 123), which lies under strong suspicion of having been garbled and, in any event, occurs in a scene which had suffered severely from the adapter's hand. This being so, and seeing that 'Duke' is the sole title employed in the 'plot' material, we conclude that 'emperor' was the Shakespearian style, 'Duke' that of the theatre and the abridger. 'Shakespeare has been guilty of no mistake in placing the emperor's court at Milan. Several of the first German emperors held their courts there occasionally' (Steevens).

28. short line.

30. *tournaments*, F. 'Turnaments;'

45–50. The broken lines at the beginning and end of this speech suggest abridgment. As F. repeats *Pro.* before l. 51, the 'cut' may have involved comments by Antonio and Panthino also, though the repetition was perhaps only due to the copyist inadvertently transcribing Antonio's cue.

84. *resembleth* To be pronounced as a quadrisyllable (Theobald). With 84–7 cf. *Son.* 33.

88. *father* F. 'Fathers.'

2. 1.

3. *but one* a quibble upon 'on'; the two words were commonly spelt alike in the 16th century.

19. *malcontent* F. 'Male-content,' which most edd. follow; but to retain the old form confuses by suggesting a quibble which was not intended.

relish a love-song v. G. 'relish.'

26. *one of the lions* 'If Shakespeare had not been thinking of the lions in the Tower, he would have written "like a lion"' (Ritson). But possibly the player pointed to the lions on a royal standard displayed in the theatre.

32. *without ye* v. note 4. 1. 3.

35. *none else would* This has puzzled many. Johnson suggested 'be so simple' understood.

73–4. *to put on your hose* Many conjectures, none satisfactory, e.g. 'put on your shoes,' 'beyond your nose,' 'put on your clothes' (cf. 'close' for 'clothes' *Ham.* 4. 5. 52). But Speed's jests are beyond inquiry.

75–6. *Belike, boy*, etc. F. prints this speech as two lines of verse; cf. note 1. 1. 133–37.

96. *servant* v. G.

128. *good-morrow, servant* F. prints 'Exit. Sil.' at the end of this line, v. p. 78.

2. 2.

It is difficult not to believe that this scene was longer in the original, and that the F. only gives us a scrap from the end. Julia is an interesting character, of whom we hear too little. 'The dialogue,' it has been observed, 'will scarcely float the action and the scene is therefore difficult to play—a very un-Shakespearian quality' (*Shak. League Journal*, Nov. 1920). Abridgment would explain the two lines of prose at the opening of a verse-scene. Cf. note 5. 3.

6. F. divides 'Why then we'll make exchange;/Here, take you this.' Possibly owing to abridgment.

14. *tide* cf. note 2. 3. 35.

19. *I come, I come* The repetition, which ruins the line of verse, was perhaps due to actor, v. p. 79 and note 4. 3. 4.

2. 3.

7. *hands;* F. 'hands,'

27. *a wood woman* (Theobald) F. 'a would-woman.'

Theobald's emendation is accepted by all mod. edd. It makes excellent sense; 'wood'=mad, with a possible reference to the wooden shoe; but it is not without difficulties. If 'wood' stood in the original, it is not easy to see how it became altered into 'would,' since the *l* of 'would' was still sounded in Shakespeare's day. Pope read 'an old woman,' and it is conceivable that Shakespeare wrote 'a nould,' an appropriate form in Launce's mouth. Another possibility is 'a wold-woman,' i.e. a country-woman.

28. *breath up and down* Perhaps in reference to the lace of the shoe. See G. 'up and down'.

29–30. *the moan she makes* Launce, we suppose, swishes the staff through the air as he says this.

34–5. *lose the tide* A tide at Verona! cf. note l. 51.

48. *In my tail!* (Hanmer) F. 'In thy Taile'; a common type of compositor's slip. For the jest cf. *Shrew* 2. 1. 215–20.

50. S.D. *he looses crab* 'lose' and 'loose' were spelt alike in the 16th century.

51. *the river* This suggests that the journey from Verona to Milan was made by river, but anyhow the river at Verona is not tidal, cf. note 1. 1. 54.

2. 4.

7. S.D. *he goes out* We follow Clark and Glover in giving Speed an exit here since he has nothing further to say in this long scene. But no motive for the exit is provided by the text, which has perhaps been tampered with by the adapter at this point in order to give Speed an entry (v. p. 81). Note that ll. 1–46 are prose, while all that follows is in verse. There is strong evidence that the prose section was originally in verse also, inasmuch as l. 36 is an isolated blank-verse line, and printed as such in the F.

19. *quote* v. G.

27. *live in your air* The chameleon was supposed to live on air.

34. *giver* v. G.

41–4. *I know it well* etc. Printed as verse in F.

47. *Now...beset* This abrupt, and (in view of 3.1.21–3) equivocal, remark is strongly suggestive of a 'cut.'

59. broken line.

60. *I know* (Hanmer) F. 'I knew'

70. *Come* (Rowe) F. 'Comes'; compositor's grammar.

83. *cite* Malone reads ''cite,' i.e. incite.

97. S.D. *Thurio goes out* v. note l. 113.

106. *a worthy mistress* (F2) F. 'a worthy a Miſtreſſe'

113. S.D. *Thurio returns* Theobald reads 'Enter Servant,' followed by mod. edd. But F. gives l. 114 to *Thur*. Note: (i) The Duke enjoins Thurio to welcome Proteus, but Thurio takes no part in the dialogue after Proteus' entry. We, therefore, give him an exit there. (ii) He cannot have been originally intended to go out and return with the Duke's message, since Silvia, after replying to the message, turns to him and bids him come with her. If the adapter 'cut' Thurio's speeches at the entry of Proteus in order to save lines and a part (i.e. the servant's), the discrepancy in the text is explained.

128. *high imperious thoughts*—a difficulty. Possibly 'thonges' stood for 'thoughts' in the original.

164. *makes* F. 'make'; compositor's grammar.

170. *dream* This use of 'dream' (again in opposition to 'dote') recurs at 4.4.79.

176–77. The extra-metrical 'Ay, and,' taken with the broken line 176, suggest a 'cut' and slight adaptation.

188. F. gives 'Exit' at the end of this line, v. p. 78.

189. *I will* Again suggestive of a 'cut.'

194. *It is mine* etc. Many attempts to emend this line, all unsatisfactory. But v. pp. 79–80.

197. *She is fair* etc. The halting rhythm of this line is suspicious.

207. *her picture* Edd. explain this as referring to

Silvia's 'outer show' as opposed to 'her mind'; but this does not fit in with l. 209 'But when I *look on her perfections.*' Note: (i) Silvia's picture is, in fact, introduced at 4. 2. (ii) Proteus' two long soliloquies come very close together in the transmitted text (cf. note 2. 5. 1). It seems possible, therefore, that 'picture' here originally meant a portrait and that this speech, in the unabridged version, was spoken before Proteus had actually met Silvia.

208. *dazzlèd* F. 'dazel'd.' The metre demands a trisyllable; cf. 1. 3. 84.

2. 5.

1. *Padua* for 'Milan.' The topography of this text is as confused as everything else about it; 'Verona' is printed for 'Milan' at 3. 1. 81 and 5. 4. 130, both in verse, where 'Milan' would be unmetrical. The confusion has been laid at Shakespeare's door; but as we cannot tell what his version contained, it is safer to attribute it to the abridger. Indeed this whole scene is so empty and formless that we can only assign it to the adapter, v. p. 81. Having brought Proteus' two soliloquies together he was obliged to pen an interval-scene of some kind, v. note 2. 4. 207.

19. *stands* v. G. 'set.'

36. *thou, that* F. 'thou that that'

44. *If thou wilt*, etc. F. has no comma. F2 reads 'If thou wilt goe with me to the Alehouſe, ſo:', which is an improvement.

49. *go to the ale* v. G. 'ale.'

2. 6.

1, 2. *forsworn?* So F. Mod. edd. omit the query and read a comma after 'Julia' and 'Silvia.' The restoration of the F. colons makes the question marks explicable. Proteus is brooding.

24. *itself:* F. 'it ſelfe,'

2. 7.

S.D. *studying a map*. At any rate it seems high time
that somebody did.

22. *fire's* a dissyllable; cf. 1. 2. 30.

30. *pilgrimage;* F. 'pilgrimage.'

32. *wide* (Collier) F. 'wilde.' Dyce follows Collier,
and they are surely right. The 'ocean' is her 'love'
where she will '*rest*, as after much turmoil/A blesséd
soul doth in Elysium.' [Note withdrawn, 1955. 'Wild' =
desert, desolate, waste (v. O.E.D. 4), is a common
epithet for the ocean.]

52. *what* Apparently some copies of F. read 'that'
(Malone).

likes So F. This form is not uncommon in Shakespeare, and is generally more euphonious than the *-est*
termination.

63. broken line.

70. *of infinite* F2 'as infinite.' Malone reads 'of the
infinite,' quoting *Ado* 2. 3. 106 'past the infinite of
thought.' Hudson reads 'o' the infinite.'

86–7. *All that is mine* etc. v. note 1. 2. 131.

3. 1.

1. Thurio's unnecessary entry and exit are perhaps
the result of an earlier portion of this scene having been
'cut.'

27. *court:* F. 'Court.'

42. *presently;* F. 'prefently.'

55. broken line.

81. *Verona* for 'Milan.' As 'Milan' will not fit the
metre, 'Verona' almost certainly was the reading of the
original version; but v. note 2. 5. 1. .

90–105. Note the rhyming couplets here; even ll.
92–3 are apparently intended to rhyme.

95. *more:* F. 'more.' 97. *you:* F. 'you.' 99. *alone:*
F. 'alone.' 101. *away:* F. 'away.'

116. *apparent* v. G.

140. F. prints the verse-letter in italics, with a space

above and below. It would not be in the Duke's 'part'
but on a separate piece of paper from which he could
read it on the stage.

141, 143, 147. *flying. lying. fortune.* So F.

149. *should be* F2, which all mod. edd. follow here,
reads 'would be.' But 'should' is more forcible.

153. *Merops' son* v. G.

170–87. *And why not death* etc. Note the strong
resemblance between this speech and *Rom.* 3. 3. 12–70
(v. pp. ix–x). The point is important; for, if Romeo's
speech (Q1), which is altogether more mature than
Valentine's, belongs as we believe to the years 1591–2,
then *The Two Gentlemen* must date from a still earlier
period.

173. *Ah! deadly* F. 'A deadly.' All edd. read 'self:
a deadly'; but the F. capital, preceded by a period,
makes it almost certain that 'ah!' is intended.

182. *to be,* F. 'to be;'

185. *to fly his deadly doom* i.e. by flying his (death's)
doom.

192. *There's not a hair* etc. The point is that Launce
has been coursing like a dog, in obedience to Proteus'
command; 'So-ho!' being the view-halloo in coursing the hare (v. Turbervile, *Booke of Hunting*, 1576,
p. 248). Launce then quibbles upon 'hair' (hare) and
'Valentine,' a valentine being a token of true-love. He
means: 'Every hair on his head proves him to be himself—
a true-love.' Valentine quibbles on his name in the same
way at ll. 211, 214.

216. *a proclamation* The issue of the proclamation,
Silvia's interview with the Duke and her committal to
prison—all are supposed to have taken place during
Valentine's soliloquy of 18 lines! It seems almost certain
that an interval-scene originally followed the soliloquy
and was cut out by the abridger. If so, the lost scene
probably concerned Julia, and perhaps dealt with her
arrival at the inn of the Host. Her appearance is very

abrupt in 4. 2., and Proteus gives a sufficiently detailed account of the palace-scene itself.

221. *banishéd* F. 'banifh'd'

263. *but one knave*. Several emendations suggested, unnecessarily. Launce is referring to the proverb, quoted by Heywood (*Proverbs*), 'Two false knaves need no broker.' Proteus being 'but one knave' needs his broker, i.e. Launce. v. G. 'broker.'

271. *catalogue* F. 'Cate-log,' which all mod. edd. follow as if it were a quibble. This is one example, out of many, of a Shakespearian spelling being retained and mistaken for a joke. 'Catelog' was formerly a recognised spelling (v. N.E.D.). Author's spellings are always liable to crop up in comic speeches because the compositor then follows his copy more closely than usual.

272. *Inprimis* We retain the F. form here and at l. 295.

279. *master's ship* (Theobald) F. 'Mastership'

280. *your old vice still* v. G. 'vice.'

290–91. *the son of thy grandmother* This jolt-head jest is unworthy of Launce.

295. *Inprimis, She can milk.* Speed should, of course, say 'Item' for 'Inprimis.' Much may lie behind this error, since it is just the kind of mistake a reviser would make in writing an addition. All the wit in this scene lies in Launce's comments upon the 'catalogue,' comments which he could have made without Speed's help. We think it possible, in short, that Speed's part in this scene was added by the adapter (v. p. 81).

296. *Ay, that she can* For the point of this and Launce's other comments, v. G. 'milk,' 'knit,' 'stock,' 'washed and scoured,' 'set the world on wheels,' 'nameless,' 'sweet mouth,' 'proud,' 'praise,' 'liberal,' 'salt.'

317. *not to be — fasting* F. 'not to be fafting.' We assume that in the original there was a blank after 'be' for the player to fill up at will; cf. 'et cetera' *Rom.* 2. 1. 38. Rowe, followed by all mod. edd., reads 'not to be kissed fasting.'

324. *slip not* (Collier) F. 'sleepe not'; cf. the pun 'ship'—'sheep' I. I. 72, 'sleppe'=slip, 'slepe'=sleep, were 16th cent. spellings (v. N.E.D.).

345. *more hair than wit* a proverbial expression. The whole speech is a parody of 'This gallant of more wit than wealth, and yet of more wealth than wisdom' (*Euphues*, p. 1).

3. 2.

3–5. *Since his exile* etc. 'From this it might be supposed that some time—days—had passed since Valentine's departure; but it is not so,' since from ll. 11–13 'it is evident that but an hour or two at the utmost can have elapsed' (Daniel, p. 122). We attribute the discrepancy to abridgment.

7. *hour's* dissyllable.

13. broken line.

24–5. broken line, with extra-metrical 'and' in following line, suggests adaptation.

46. *You have prevailed* Proteus' consent, after ll. 39–41, is somewhat suddenly given; possibly the Duke's argument was longer in the original.

49. *weed* We suggest *wend*, i.e. to make to wind. Possibly mistaken for 'wead' (a minim-misprint, v. T.I. p. xli). Thurio continues the metaphor.

71. *Ay* Either actor's gag, or relic of a 'cut.'

77. *such integrity* 'Such' is left in mid-air, while 'Orpheus' lute' is irrelevant as the passage stands. It is possible to defend this as a violent aposiopesis, but in a text like the present a 'cut' provides the best explanation. Malone writes 'I suspect that a line following this has been lost.' Cf. p. 79.

91. *Let us* etc. Halting rhythm suggests adaptation.

95. broken line.

4. 1.

This is the first of the forest scenes, which were certainly longer and probably more numerous in the original version, since nowhere else is the adapter's knife busier or more evident. Note (i) the irrational mingling of verse and prose in the present scene; (ii) the poor quality of much of the 'verse'; e.g. ll. 5, 40, 73.

3. *about ye* We fancy that the form 'ye' may have been a favourite of the adapter. Bartlett gives more instances of its use in this text than in any other.

10. *he's* (Capell) F. 'he is'

21. *sixteen months* 'The sixteen months is not wanted for the plot of the play' (Daniel, p. 122); but they may have been needed in the original version.

27. *I killed a man* The abridged text gives no reason for Valentine's falsehood.

34–5. This is surely too poor to be Shakespeare.

35. *often had been* (F3) F. 'often had beene often'

49. *near allied* (Theobald) F. 'Neece, alide' A minim-error; 'neere' taken for 'neece.' The converse mistake is found in *John* 2. 1. 424.

55–8. *And partly...much want* The absence of a finite verb in this sentence may be accounted for by a 'cut.'

56. *shape,* F. 'ſhape;'

64. *consórt* Note that this word is 'cónsort' at 3. 2. 84.

74. *crew* F. 'Crewes'; compositor's grammar.

4. 2.

There is no change of place in this and the two following scenes, and we have, therefore, treated them as one scene, which indeed is how they must have been played according to the received text. Such continuity of treatment, however, involves difficulties of time, as we shall note below, and it seems likely that at least one scene, i.e. between 4. 3. and 4. 4., has been lost.

Daniel notes that while at first sight 4. 2. appears to take place on the same day as 3. 2. in which Thurio announces his intention to serenade Silvia, this cannot be so, because (i) the duke first gives Proteus permission to have access to Silvia in 3. 2., while the opening words of 4. 2. show that he has been visiting her for some time, days at least; (ii) since 2. 7. stands between two scenes both occurring on the day of Valentine's banishment, Julia must have set out from Verona on that day, and it is impossible that she could have arrived the same night at Milan. Adaptation explains all these anomalies.

1–2. These two lines appear to be not only completely different in quality from those which follow, but hardly to be described as verse at all.

25. *tune,* F. 'tune:'

26. *Now, my young guest* etc. The Host-Julia parts of this scene, like the outlaw-scenes, have evidently been greatly adapted. Note: (i) the mixture of verse and prose; e.g. ll. 26–7, 54, 70–1, 135–6 are lines of verse, and so printed in the F. (ii) the F. prints some of the prose as lines or half-lines of verse, which suggests that the copy from which the 'parts' were derived had been revised.

allicholy Mistress Quickly makes the same mistake, *M.W.W.* 1. 4. 148.

59–60. F. divides 'Not ſo; but yet/So falſe that he grieves my very heart-ſtrings.'

83, 86. broken lines.

91. *man!* F. 'man:'

108. *Valentine is dead.* Daniel notes that this lie would lack even the merit of plausibility if the scene took place on the same day as Valentine's banishment.

109. *his grave* (F2) F. 'her graue'

114. broken line.

117. *hanging in your chamber* Proteus' knowledge of the picture suggests that he has had access to Silvia's chamber before this scene. But cf. note 2. 4. 207.

4. 3.

4. *Madam, madam!* The repetition ruins the line of verse, but may be explained as actor's gag or careless copying of the 'part.'

13. The actor or adapter appears to have added 'wise'; without it the line runs well.

17. *abhors* (Hanmer) F. 'abhor'd'

23. *Mantua* cf. 5. 2. 47. But 'Mantua' may be part of the general topographical confusion of the text.

43–4. *At Friar Patrick's cell* etc. These words appear to be borrowed from 5. 2. 41–2 or vice versa.

45–6. Note that the scene suddenly drops into prose.

4. 4.

It is clear from 'That's her chamber' (l. 84) that we are still at the foot of Silvia's tower, as in 4. 3. But, while Eglamour departs at dawn, Launce does not come on until the Duke has at least begun his dinner, i.e. after noon, the Elizabethan dining-hour. We may, therefore, feel tolerably certain that a scene has been cut out between 4. 3. and 4. 4., perhaps one dealing with Valentine's life with the outlaws.

17. *the duke's table* cf. note 1. 3. 27. Yet this speech must be Shakespearian. Possibly 'duke' was intended as a comic error on Launce's part, like 'Prodigious son.' If so, this may explain how 'duke' got into the 'plot' material.

33. *Madam Silvia* Warburton read 'Madam Julia,' with some plausibility, since at any rate on the occasion of which Launce has just been speaking 'the fellow that whips the dogs' allowed him no opportunity for taking formal leave of Silvia.

40. *I will do* (Malone) F. 'ile doe'

42. *two days* Yet, as the text stands, the impression (which is everything in the theatre) we gather is that Proteus arrived in Milan only one day. before these words were uttered. v. head-note to 4. 2.

45. *Jewel* We retain the F. capital, which perhaps denotes the dog's name.

52–5. *Ay sir, the other squirrel* etc. Arranged as four verse-lines in F., cf. note 1. 1. 133–37.

53. *hangman boys* (Singer) F. 'Hangmans boyes' F2 reads 'Hangmans boy' v. G.

67. *know thou* (F2) F. 'know thee' The abruptness of this line is suspicious.

71. *nor love* (Johnson) F. 'not leave' F2 reads 'to leaue' which most edd. follow. But Johnson's reading makes better sense, and 'loue' might easily be confused with 'leue'; cf. note 1. 1. 65.

73–6. *Alas!...thou pity her?* Mod. edd. arrange these lines as 'verse'; but 'I cannot choose but pity her' is printed as prose in F. and the dialogue is probably a prose patch due to abridgment.

84. *That's her chamber* This abrupt parenthesis, which alone marks the place where the dialogue occurs, is we fancy an addition by the adapter. The foregoing line halts badly, and the original may have read

...give her that ring,
And therewithal this letter: Tell my lady

105. S.D. *Silvia comes from the postern.* The received text necessitates an entry here for Silvia; yet the following dialogue clearly should take place in Silvia's chamber, since at l.115 she bids Ursula fetch the picture and without a pause hands it to Julia. Such a sudden change of scene is of course possible on the Elizabethan stage, but there is a strong probability that it was here due not to Shakespeare but to the adapter who ran two scenes into one in order to save lines. The prose at ll. 111–115 and the broken lines at ll. 125, 136–7, 140, 146, 155 support this.

147–8. *than she is;/...loved her well*, F. 'then she is,/... lou'd her well;' transposing the terminal pointing. Cf. *Tempest* note 2. 1. 165–6.

165. *Madam, 'twas Ariadne* The abrupt 'Madam' suggests tampering.

5. 1.

One suspects abridgment in this very short scene, but there are no obvious indications of it.

5. 2.

Note that this scene falls into two parts: (i) ll. 1–30, before the Duke's entry, in which the dialogue is a mixture of verse and prose; (ii) the remainder—all verse. The prose is perhaps abridged verse.

5. *too little* Proteus is quibbling upon 'leg'; but his meaning is obscure, perhaps because the jest is abridged.

7. *Julia* (Boswell) These asides (cf. ll. 13, 18, 21, 24, 28) all clearly belong to one character, and F. gives them to Julia, except this one, which it assigns to Proteus, and ll. 13–14 which it assigns to Thurio. In stringing together players' parts the name-indicators would be peculiarly liable to confusion in rapid dialogue like this.

9. *fair* i.e. Thurio is 'fair-faced'=a specious deceiver.

13. *pearls* v. G.

20. *she makes no doubt of that* i.e. she knows all about that.

26. *pities them* v. G. 'possessions.'

32. *saw Sir Eglamour* (F2) F. 'faw Eglamoure'

34. *Why then* F. prints as separate line.

5. 3.

Another outlaw-scene, clearly abridged, cf. Introd. p. xvi. Note: (i) the mixture of prose and verse; (ii) the cowardice of Eglamour (v. pp. xvi–xvii); (iii) the opening speech in F. 'Come, come be patient:/We must bring you to our Captaine,' which looks like a makeshift introduction (cf. 2. 2.), borrowed from l. 12 below, previous matter dealing with the capture of Silvia having been deleted.

7. *Moses* F. 'Moyfes'—a 16th cent. form, used by Tyndale. Perhaps the original text had more to tell us of 'Moses and Valerius.'

5. 4.

This scene, a 'damned spot,' as it stands, upon Shakespeare's dramatic reputation, has long been suspected of serious corruption. Cf. Introd. pp. xiii–xix. After the foregoing analysis of the text as a whole, the reader will, we hope, be prepared to agree that the matter has passed beyond conjecture into certainty. Distinct scenes in Shakespeare's original, we believe, went to the manufacture of this, the adapter's masterpiece. Dramatically and metrically it falls into three sections: (i) Valentine's soliloquy, followed by Proteus' attempted violence upon Silvia which is interrupted by Valentine. All this, though not free from 'cuts,' is in the simple end-stopped verse which we associate with the youthful Shakespeare. (ii) The repentance of Proteus, Valentine's strange surrender of Silvia, and the incident of Julia's swoon and the ring. This section is in quite another style, marked by enjambment, strong medial pauses and—strange combination!—a riot of rhymed couplets, mingled with scraps of prose, in one of which (v. note l. 89) we find a fossil line of blank-verse. Further it contains passages which approach perilously near to nonsense, e.g. ll. 71–2, 107–10, 113–16. From the remarkable silence of Silvia, while events so vital to her happiness were proceeding (v. p. xviii), we may suppose that the adapter was here availing himself of hints from a Shakespearian scene between Valentine, Proteus and Julia, at which Silvia was not present. But, if so, they were hints only, for we can hardly doubt that the section as it has reached us is virtually his own composition. (iii) In the third section, which begins with the entry of the Duke and Thurio, we return to the style of the young Shakespeare. This section may have been taken from a later portion of the scene which commenced in section (i). On the other hand, it may have been located in Verona (v. note l. 130). We cannot tell. One of the minor problems of the scene is the fate of Speed, who was captured with Valentine in 4. 1. but does not appear here, v. p. 81.

2. *This shadowy desert* etc. Collier suggested 'These shadowy, desert,' etc. which is probably right.

47–9. *For whose dear sake* etc. Clearly corrupt. Daniel proposed 'discandied' for 'descended' and a full-stop after 'perjury.' Possibly 'rend thy' should be read 'candy' likewise.

58. *force ye* The repetition in l. 59, the use of 'ye' (v. note 4. 1. 3), and the metre—all point to the adapter as author of this line.

62–121. This forms the middle, and most corrupt, section of the scene. Note that it would just about take up one side of a foolscap sheet.

67. *trusted, when one's own right hand* (Johnson) F. 'truſted, when one's right hand.' F2 'truſted now, when one's right hand,' which most edd. follow, despite the echo of 'now' in l. 65. The passage is strong enough for Shakespeare, and the error perhaps originated through careless copying by the adapter.

71–2. *The private wound* etc. Many attempts have been made to mend the metre of these lines. The sense needs mending also.

73. short line. Note 'confounds' for 'confound'

84–98. *O me, unhappy* etc. We print this medley of verse-scraps and adapter's prose as it stands in the F. It is idle to try and bring order into it.

87. *Why wag!* Curious language for Valentine who had never seen 'Sebastian' before.

89–90. *which, out of my neglect, was never done* A line of verse, embedded in a prose speech! The adapter is caught—in the act. Cf. p. 80.

107–10. *if shame live…minds* Verse and sense leave little doubt as to the authorship of these lines.

113–16. *makes him run…constant eye* Also patently adapter's composition, cf. Introd. p. xvii. Note that 'all th'sins' is not Shakespearian. Shakespeare never contracts the definite article before a consonant, except when it is preceded by a preposition, e.g. by th', i'th', o'th', etc.

123. *Forbear* etc. This long line also may be given to the adapter, with little hesitation, as part of the stitch-work between sections (ii) and (iii). Note that it is the only line of 'verse' in the text in which the word 'duke' appears; cf. note 1. 3. 27.

126. *Silvia's mine* The jingle 'Valentine'—'mine' is strongly suggestive of the adapter with his passion for couplets.

130. *Verona shall not hold thee* v. note 2. 5. 1; but this dialogue may have taken place in Verona in the original. Theobald suggests 'Milan shall not behold thee'; possibly 'hold' = ''hold.'

144. *repeal thee home* This also is curious. Milan was not Valentine's 'home.'

145. *Plead a new state* v. G. 'state.'

157. *reforméd, civil, full of good* This description agrees with 4. 1. 71–3 and 5. 3. 13–14, but certainly not with 5. 4. 15–17, 20–1.

THE STAGE-HISTORY OF
THE TWO GENTLEMEN OF VERONA

The Two Gentlemen of Verona has not been a favourite in the theatre. Meres mentions it in *Palladis Tamia* (1598); but the earliest performance of which record remains is that presented by Garrick at Drury Lane on December 22, 1762; and this, according to Genest, was the first time the play had been given in that theatre. Garrick acted no character in the play; and the production was not Shakespeare's play, but a clumsy alteration of it by Benjamin Victor, Treasurer of Drury Lane Theatre, who made confusion of the plot by altering the arrangement of certain scenes, and wrote additional matter for the last act in order to bring the comic characters, Launce and Speed, on the stage again. The sixth repetition of this play, on January 25, 1763, saw the outbreak of the 'Half-Price Riots.' On this and the following evening Drury Lane Theatre was wrecked by a gang headed by 'Thady' Fitzpatrick; and John Moody, who was acting the Host, only saved the scenery from being set on fire by dragging the incendiary forcibly away. The first recorded performance of the play at Covent Garden took place on April 13, 1784; the production appears to have been Shakespeare's play, with some slight alterations; and three representations of Shakespeare's play were given by John Philip Kemble at Drury Lane in January, 1790. On April 21, 1808, however, Kemble, at Covent Garden, fell back on Victor's version, of which he retained some of the worst features, and added to it some lines of his own composition. In this production Kemble himself played Valentine. The production was not liked and was given only three times. The stage fortunes of the play reached their low-water mark when Charles Kemble had it 'degraded' by Fredcric Reynolds into a spectacular opera, the music being produced at Covent Garden on November 29, 1821. At the third performance, when a 'Palace of the Hours, and the Temple of Apollo' were introduced for the first time, various mishaps with the elaborate scenery filled the evening with hearty mirth; but the spectacle survived this trial and was given twenty-nine times. There is mention of a performance of Shakespeare's play at Bath on March 23, 1822. Macready gave the play, according to the received text, at Drury Lane on December 29, 1841; Charles Kean in England and America in the eighteen-forties, and Samuel Phelps at Sadler's Wells in the eighteen-fifties. Of recent years the only productions have been that by Osmund Tearle at the Shakespeare Festival, Stratford-upon-Avon, in 1890, by Augustin Daly (with Ada Rehan as Julia) in New York and London in 1895, and by J. H. Leigh at the Court Theatre, London, in April 1904, with Acton Bond as Valentine.

[1921]   HAROLD CHILD

GLOSSARY

Note. Where a pun or quibble is intended the meanings are distinguished as (*a*), (*b*), etc.

AGOOD, in good earnest; 4. 4. 163

AIMED AT, guessed at, hinted at; 3. 1. 45

ALE, 'go to the ale with a Christian.' A reference to 'Church-ale,' a parish festival; 2. 5. 49

ALLICHOLY, i.e. melancholy; 4. 2. 26

ALONE, peerless; 2. 4. 165

AN-END, perpetually; 4. 4. 59

APPARENT, obvious, evident (i.e. almost the opposite of the modern meaning, v. *Shak. Eng.* ii. 563); 3. 1. 116

AWFUL, i.e. commanding respect; 4. 1. 46

BEADSMAN, one who tells beads, or prays, for another; 1. 1. 18

BEAR WITH YOU, (*a*) endure, (*b*) maintain, support, v. *letter*; 1. 1. 117–18

BID THE BASE, v. note; 1. 2. 97

BOOTS, 'give me not the boots,' i.e. don't make game of me; 1. 1. 27

BOTTOM, a bottom was the core of the skein upon which the wool was wound; 3. 2. 53

BROKER, pander, go-between; 1. 2. 42

CHANGE, modulation; 4. 2. 66

CIRCUMSTANCE, (*a*) evidence, argument, (*b*) condition; 1. 1. 36, 37, 82

CODPIECE (to stick pins on), part of male attire made indelicately conspicuous in Shakespeare's time; 2. 7. 56. Cf. Jack of Newbury 'a great cod peece, whereon he stuck his pins' (*Deloney's Works*, Oxford, p. 27)

COLD (for catching), i.e. 'lest they should catch cold' with a quibble upon 'colled' or 'culled' = embraced; 1. 2. 136

COMMENDATIONS, remembrances; 1. 3. 53

COMPETITOR, partner, confederate; 2. 6. 35. Cf. 'the rivals of my watch' *Ham.* 1. 1. 13

CONCEITLESS, dull, lacking in imagination; 4. 2. 92

CONSORT, company (generally of musicians); 3. 2. 84; 4. 1. 64

CURST, i.e. a shrew; 3. 1. 335

DESCANT, v. note 1. 2. 80–97; 1. 2. 94

DIRECTION-GIVER, one who directs an archer's aim, cf. *gave aim to*; 3. 2. 90

DISCIPLINE, instruction; 3. 2. 88

DOG, 'to be a dog at' = to be expert; 4. 4. 12

DRIFT, plot, intention; 2. 6. 43; 3. 1. 18; 4. 2. 79

DUCAT, i.e. about 3/6, v. note; 1. 1. 134

DUMP, plaintive melody or song (v. *Sh. Eng.* ii. 442); 3. 2. 85

EARNEST, money paid as an instalment (quibble); 2. 1. 150

ENDING ANTHEM, requiem; 3. 1. 240

EVE'S LEGACY, v. *proud*; 3. 1. 331

EXCEPT, (*a*) find fault with, (*b*) leave out of account; 1. 3. 83; 5. 2. 3

EXHIBITION, maintenance allowance; 1. 3. 69

EYE (be in), i.e. be within range of; 1. 3. 32

FAIR, v. note; 5. 2. 9

FISH, 'as whole as a fish'; 2. 5. 17. 'Fish-whole' (v. N.E.D.) = 'thoroughly sound and healthy,' but Launce probably intends an indelicate reference as well, cf. 'fish-monger' *Ham.* 2. 2. 174

GAVE AIM TO, i.e. acted as 'direction-giver' (q.v.). Here the archer, of course, treacherously shoots at the 'giver' instead of the target; 5. 4. 102. Halliwell quotes Webster, *White Devil*, 3. 1. 25, 'I am at the mark, sir: I'll give aim to you,/And tell you how near you shoot.'

GIVER, i.e. 'direction-giver' (q.v.); 2. 4. 34

GOSSIPS, i.e. female friends invited to be present at a birth (N.E.D.), or god-parents for a child (here illegitimate); 3. 1. 268

HAMMER, i.e. in the brain; 1. 3. 18

HANGMAN, i.e. fit for the hangman. Cf. O.E.D. 1 b; 'hangman boy', *Golden Ass* 1566 [Loeb ed. p. 329, l. 8]; 4. 4. 53

HARD-FAVOURED, ugly; 2. 1. 46

IMPOSE, injunction; 4. 3. 8

INFLUENCE, i.e. of a star, in the astrological sense; 3. 1. 183

INLY, i.e. intimate, heartfelt; 2. 7. 18

INTERPRET, to expound the meaning of a puppet-show; 2. 1. 91

JADE, vicious or ill-conditioned mare or woman; 3. 1. 274

KILL, i.e. subdue; 1. 2. 69

KNIT, with a quibble upon 'knit' meaning 'conceive' (v. N.E.D. 'knit' 4 d.); 3. 1. 302

LACED MUTTON, cant term for a courtesan; 'laced' possibly refers to a slashed bodice, with a pun on 'lace' i.e. to make incisions on the breast of a bird before cooking (v. N.E.D.); 1. 1. 95

LEASE (out by), (*a*) let out to others, (*b*) = leash (16th cent. spelling 'leasse')—so 'out of control,' v. *possessions*; 5. 2. 29

LETTER (very orderly), possibly with a quibble upon 'letter' = one who lets rooms, i.e. a landlady. If so, 'very orderly' may be a reference to an advertisement posted in the window of such apartments. Cf. '*bear with you*'; 1. 1. 119

LIBERAL, i.e. loose in her talk; 3. 1. 340

LUMPISH, low-spirited; 3. 2. 62

MANAGE, wield, 3. 1. 247

MEAN, v. note 1. 2. 80–97; 1. 2. 95

MEROPS' SON, Phaethon was the son of Phoebus and Clymene, wife of Merops. The Duke, in contempt of Valentine's birth, refuses to call him the son of Phoebus. Possibly a pun on 'ropes' (i.e. the ladder of cord) may be intended also; 3. 1. 153

MILK, Launce takes 'milk' in the sense of 'entice by wiles.' Cf.

Fletcher *Rule a Wife*, 2. 4.
'All this is but seeming to milk
the lover on' (N.E.D.); 3.1.295

MONTH'S MIND, i.e. a strong in-
clination (orig. a mass said a
month after the death of a person); 1. 2. 137

MOTION, puppet-show; 2. 1. 90

NAMELESS, inexpressible; 3. 1. 311

NICE, i.e. as we should say 'particular'; 3. 1. 82

NICK (out of all), i.e. beyond all
computation; 4. 2. 73

NODDY, simpleton, or (adj.) foolish;
1. 1. 110, 113, 120

NOTE, v. note; 1. 2. 80–97

ORDERLY, v. *letter*; 1. 1. 119

OVER-SHOES, OVER-BOOTS, phrases
'expressing reckless continuance
in a course already begun'
(N.E.D.), derived of course
from wading through water or
mire. Leander was 'over-shoes'
in the Hellespont; Proteus was
'over-boots' in the mire of love.
Cf. *Rom.* 1. 4. 41 'the mire of
this sir-reverence love'; 1. 1.
24, 25

OWE, own; 5. 2. 28

PEARLS, cataracts; 5. 2. 13

PINFOLD, pound for stray cattle;
1. 1. 105

PLEAD A NEW STATE, v. *state*; 5. 4.
145

POSSESSIONS, with a quibble on
'possession' by a spirit; 5. 2.
25

POST, (*a*) stock, (*b*) courier, messenger; 1. 1. 149

PRAISE, appraise, i.e. sip; 3. 1. 337

PRETENCE, intention; 3. 1. 47

PRETENDED, v. *pretence*; 2. 6. 37

PRINCIPALITY, a spiritual being of
a high rank; 2. 4. 150

PRINT (in), precisely; 2. 1. 161

PRODIGIOUS, mistake for 'Prodigal';
2. 3. 3

PROPORTION, mistake for 'portion';
2. 3. 3

PROUD, Launce takes 'proud' in
the sense of 'hot-blooded,' 'lascivious.' Cf. *Lucrece*, 712 'The
flesh being proud, Desire doth
fight with grace'; 3. 1. 330

PUDDINGS, guts of an animal; 4.
4. 29

QUAINTLY, cunningly; 2. 1. 117;
3. 1. 117

QUIPS, retorts; 4. 2. 12

QUOTE, observe, note—with a
quibble on 'coat,' 'quote' being
pronounced and often spelt as
'cote'; 2. 4. 18, 19

RECORD, sing, warble; 5. 4. 6

RELISH, sing, warble; 2. 1. 19

REPEAL, recall from exile; 3. 1.
234; 5. 4. 144

ROAD, roadstead; 1. 1. 53; 2. 4.
185

ST NICHOLAS, the patron saint of
scholars; 3. 1. 293

SALT, with a quibble upon 'salt'
meaning 'wit'; 3. 1. 353

SEARCH, probe a wound as with a
surgeon's knife; 1. 2. 116

SERVANT, one devoted to the service of a lady, who was not
pledged by accepting it; 2. 1.
96; 2. 4. 1, 103–5

SET, i.e. set to music, v. note; 1.
2. 80–97

SET, i.e. 'put down,' with an indelicate allusion (cf. 2. 5. 19–
20); 2. 1. 81

SET THE WORLD ON WHEELS, 'to let things slide, enjoy myself' (cf. *Ant. and Cleop.* 2. 7. 96–8); 3. 1. 309

SHOT, tavern-reckoning; 2. 5. 5, 7

SILLY, helpless; 4. 1. 72

SINEWS, nerves; 3. 2. 78

SLOW, heavy; 4. 2. 63

SO-HO, v. note; 3. 1. 192

SORT, select; 3. 2. 92

STATE, 'plead a new state,' a term of rhetoric. State = 'the point in question or debate between contending parties, as it emerges from their pleadings' (N.E.D. 'state' 12); 5. 4. 145

STOCK (with a wench), dowry; 3. 1. 303

SUN-EXPELLING MASK, 'Much worn by ladies of quality when riding; the eyeholes at times were filled with glass' (*Sh. Eng.* ii. 97); 4. 4. 151

SWEET MOUTH (she hath a), i.e. she is wanton, lecherous. Launce takes it literally; 3. 1. 321

SWINGED, thrashed (with a quibble perhaps at 2. 1. 78, cf. *M.W.W.* 5. 5. 197); 2. 1. 78; 3. 1. 371

TABLE, tablet for memoranda; 2. 7. 3

TAKEN UP, scolded, rebuked; 1. 2. 135

TENDER, have regard for; 4. 4. 138

TESTERNED, 'tipped' with a tester, i.e. sixpence; 1. 1. 141

TIMELESS, untimely; 3. 1. 21

TUNE, v. note, 1. 2. 80–97; 1. 2. 88, 89

TURN, be inconstant; 2. 2. 4

UNGARTERED, to go ungartered was a conventional sign of the love-lorn swain; 2. 1. 69

UP AND DOWN, exactly, for all the world (cf. *Ado*, 2. 1. 107) 2. 3. 28

URINAL, physician's glass for testing the patient's water; 2. 1. 37

VALENTINE, true-love token; 3. 1. 192, 214

VICE, 'your old vice still' with a quibble upon 'vice' the iniquity clown of the old moralities; 3. 1. 280

WASHED AND SCOURED, i.e. knocked down and beaten. 'Wash' is a Shakespearian form of 'swash' (cf. *Rom.* 1. 1. 69) and 'to scour' = to beat (cf. *Hen. V.* 2. 1. 60); 3. 1. 307

WATER-SPANIEL; 3. 1. 270; for the 'qualities' of this animal cf. 4. 2. 14

WELL-DERIVED, (a) well-born, (b) i.e. a 'great come-down'; 5. 2. 23

WELL-FAVOURED, (a) gracious (cf. 2. 1. 52), (b) beloved; 2.11. 47, 50

WOOD WOMAN, v. note; 2. 3. 27

YKT, this word clearly had some comic significance now lost (cf. *Ant. and Cleo.* 2. 5. 49; *Temp.* 2. 1. 40); 2. 1. 110, 115